ACKNOWLEDGEMENTS

I wish to thank the following people

Ruth Sheldrick and Kate Davey, for the illustrations.

Alison Brookes, for proof reading.

Brighton Children's Library for helping me in some of my research for the book.

The Nina West Nurseries, in London, who tried out and provided some of the practical ideas.

All the friends who have helped to promote the Open-Sez-Me books.

WITHDRAWN

OPEN-SEZ-ME

FOREWORD

'THE MAGIC OF PLEASANT DISCOVERIES'

Seasons come, seasons go... the cycle of nature still continues.

AUTUMN is the last in the series of four OPEN-SEZ-ME books, which are set in each of the seasons. And, like the seasons, these books are full of "The Magic of Pleasant Discoveries," opening the door to many new ideas, activities and festivals.

The festivals in particular reflect a wide variety of religions. My aim is to offer children the opportunity to develop a wider understanding and appreciation of their own culture and those of others... to enhance their exploration and enjoyment of the world around them, and the people they share it with!

Shirley West

CONTENTS

SEPTEMBER

SEPTEMBER

COOKING   PAGE

STORIES AND SONGS

POEMS

OCTOBER

FACTS   PAGE

OCTOBER

STORIES AND SONGS PAGE

POEMS

NOVEMBER

COOKING   PAGE

STORIES AND SONGS

POEMS

SEPTEMBER

'Warm September brings the fruit;
Sportsmen then begin to shoot.'

Although September is the ninth month
of the year, its name comes from the
Latin '**septum**' meaning seven. Its origin
was from the Roman calendar.

WHAT SEPTEMBER BRINGS

In September the weather is still warm, but the days are shorter and the nights are longer.

Many insects die in September. Before they die, they lay their eggs. The female of the green grasshopper lays her eggs underground through a long tube which looks like a tail. The daddy-long-legs also lays its eggs underground.

The female earwig doesn't die in autumn. She lays 20-40 eggs in a little hollow in the ground and looks after the eggs all winter.

The black and red beetles bury their eggs next to food such as a dead mouse so that when the eggs hatch the larvae can eat.

Walking through the garden in September, you'll be able to find lots of spider's webs. These webs are spiders' homes and are also used for catching insects.

Hedgehogs usually have two litters in a year, one about midsummer and another in August/ September. In late autumn, hedgehogs find a snug nest under dead leaves in which to hibernate - but they wake up in warm spells and go out to find some food.

Quite a few smaller mammals - such as hares, dormice, bats, and shrews - survive the winter by hibernating. This means they eat plenty of food during the summer and autumn to build up reserves of fat, then dig a burrow, and spend the coldest weather in a deep sleep underground.

THE ARRIVAL OF AUTUMN

Autumn is the season of harvesting, and beautiful colouring, and starts on the 23rd of September. This is the season when farmers all over the world gather in their crops and store them for use during the winter.

Falling leaves are the most obvious sign that Autumn has arrived, and in the USA this season is known as the Fall. Trees lose water through their leaves, so, by shedding them in Autumn, they are able to slow down their growth. This way they survive throughout Winter when the ground is frozen and their roots cannot draw up sap.

AUTUMN TIME

All the leaves are falling down,
Dancing, swirling to the ground,
Bright, gleaming and golden brown
There is a stillness about the town.

Autumn leaves make bonfires red,
Bonfires burning till they're dead.
Down goes Guy's fallen head,
Party's over and off to bed.

All the trees are brown and bare,
Autumn's come I do declare.
Burning smells are in the air,
And warmer clothes we have to wear!

By Shirley West

THINGS TO DO

LEAF TILES

<u>YOU WILL NEED</u>

2 cups of plain flour, 1 cup salt, 1 cup water, 2 tablespoons cooking oil, a rolling pin, leaves.

Oven temperature: 130' C/250'F/Gas 1/2

<u>METHOD</u>

1. Mix all the ingredients together to form a dough. Roll out with a rolling pin until it is 2 cm (1") thick.

2. Press the leaf, vein side down, onto the dough so that it leaves a mark. Remove the leaf and bake in the oven for two hours.

LEAF PRINTING

<u>YOU WILL NEED</u>

Dry leaves, paper, crayons, chip wallpaper.

<u>METHOD</u>

1. Remove the leafy part of the leaf leaving the vein. Glue this to a piece of paper.

2. Take a whole leaf and glue it next to the other leaf. Place a piece of paper on top and rub with a crayon. Cut out the leaves.

3. Draw a large tree without leaves on the chip paper and crayon the bark in brown. Glue the leaves to the tree.

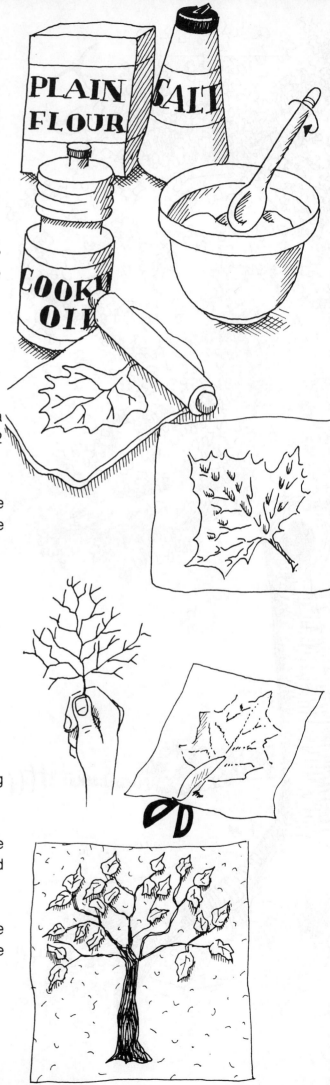

PRESERVING AUTUMN LEAVES

YOU WILL NEED

A small fallen brach with leaves, jam jar, glycerine, water.

METHOD

1. Split the woody stem about 8 cm (3') up and stand it in a jam jar of warm water and glycerine for a few hours.

2. Leaves that curl must be cut off as they will not last.

PINE CONES

Cones develop from the female flower. After pollination, the scales harden and close. The stalk often bends, so the cone hangs down. The cone turns from green to brown, and when the seeds are ripe and the weather is warm and dry, the scales open. The seeds flutter out on papery wings.

YOU WILL NEED

Several pine cones, water.

METHOD

1. Submerge the cone pine in some water, the scales will close.

2. Then place it in a warm place and it will open.

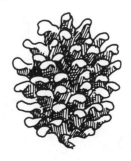

MAKING PLASTER CASTS OF TRACKS

If you can find a good clear track, you can make a plaster cast of it.

YOU WILL NEED

Card, plaster of Paris, paint, varnish, paper-clip, water.

METHOD

1. Bend a strip of strong card, 30 cm (1 ft) wide, into a circle and join the ends together with a paper clip.

2. Remove leaves and bits of twig around the track. Push the card ring into the ground to surround it.

3. Mix the plaster of Paris and water together in a bowl. Stir to a paste.

4. Pour the paste into the ring near the edge. Tap the ring to remove any air bubbles.

5. Allow at least 20 minutes to set. Lift up the cast with a knife and gently remove the ring.

6. Clean the finished cast under a tap. Paint and allow to dry before giving it a coat of clear varnish.

1.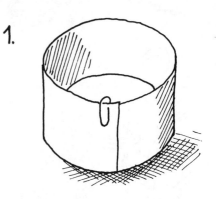

3.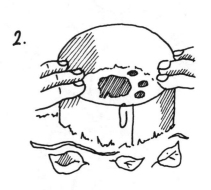

4.

6. 5.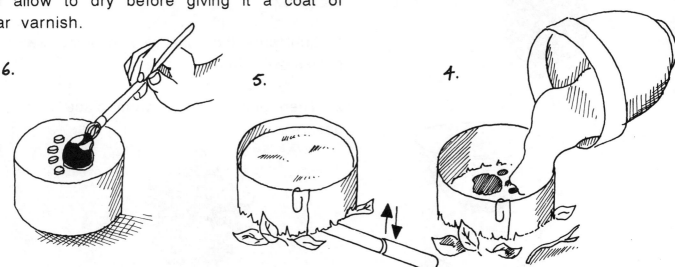

SLUGS AND SNAILS

Slugs and snails are the same kind of animal. They both have a single foot that can travel on a coating of slime and they both need moisture to live. Both have a lung and breathe air and both eat, digest and reproduce in similar ways. A quick distinction between these molluscs is that snails have shells which are made up of a chalky substance but slugs have not.

Snails have a breathing tube on the right hand side of their body, just under the edge of their shell, and this can be seen when they are extended. Slugs have a breathing aperture, just on the edge of the mantel which is the raised hump on their back, covering the lung.

Some snails, breathe air through simple sac-like lungs. Others which breathe in water, have fringes of leaf-like gills, similar to those of fish.

Snails cut or shred their food by means of a peculiar ribbon-like apparatus, the '**radula**' (Latin word meaning '**little file**'), which is in the mouth and studded with minute teeth.

A snail has two pairs of tentacles on its head. The larger pair has eyes on the tips. The smaller tentacles are used for smelling. If one of these creatures loses an '**eye-horn**' it grows another. And a snail can crawl across the edge of a razor without cutting itself!

Like snails, slugs are both male and female. But eggs are laid only after two slugs have mated. The eggs are laid in the soil and will hatch about three weeks later. The baby slugs are able to feed straightaway and they grow quickly.

THINGS TO DO

DISCOVERING SNAILS

<u>YOU WILL NEED</u>

Some snails and slugs, black paper, green leaves, nail varnish.

<u>METHOD</u>

1. Collect some snails and slugs from the garden and place them on the black paper with the green leaves. Now watch the slimy tracks they make on the paper, and watch them eat.

2. Before returning the snails safely to the garden number each one with some nail varnish. Have a look the next morning and see if the same snails have returned to the garden.

KEEPING SLUGS AND SNAILS

Snails and slugs can be kept in a variety of containers. There should be air holes in the top of the container, but the air must always be damp for the animals to be active. It's great fun seeing how the slugs and snails move along the wall of the tank.

<u>YOU WILL NEED</u>

Some snails and slugs, soil, small pieces of turf, an old fish tank.

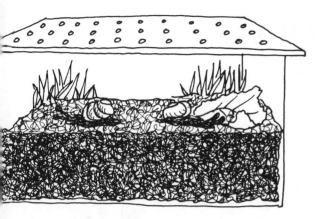

METHOD

1. Put at least 8 cm (3') of moist soil at the bottom of the fish tank. Place the turf on top.

2. Collect no more than two or three snails or slugs from the garden and place them in the tank.

3. Feed the snails with mashed potato, cabbage or lettuce leaves. Slugs prefer fresh cabbage, lettuce leaves, and carrots. Remove any stale food each day and clean the tank every two or three weeks.

SLUGS AND SNAILS

Slugs and snails are very sticky,
And picking slugs up can be tricky.
Slugs and snails are very slow,
Follow their trail and see where they go.

Snails have houses on their backs,
And very seldom have to pack.
While slugs, they have no house at all,
And make their home within a wall.

So into the garden you must go,
To watch these creatures keeping low.
Feeding on leaves and everything in sight,
And leaving trails that are ever so white.

By Shirley West

KITE FLYING FESTIVAL

Between 1st and 9th September

This festival comes on the ninth day of the ninth moon, or month, by the Chinese calendar. A week or so before the festival, stores display kites of all kinds and sizes. Children make their own kites, using bamboo sticks for the lightweight frames, and then spreading paper across the frame.

On the morning of the festival, strange and beautiful kites can be seen filling the skies. At the end of the day everyone lets go of their kite and anyone who finds a kite after it has fallen to the ground should burn it.

The Chinese people believe that, long ago, the first kite to appear in China was flown by a man called Han Shin, a clever dwarf. He was supposed to have used this first kite in a unique way to win a battle for his country. They remember him to this day by flying kites shaped like him.

TWO CHILDREN

Two little children went out one day.
Into the park in order to play.
They took with them two kites to fly,
A great big centipede, and a butterfly.
Then up on the hill their kites sailed high.
Ducking and diving in the September sky.

By Shirley West.

Suggested Songs: **Kite Flying High**, from **Flying A Round**, published by A. C. Black.

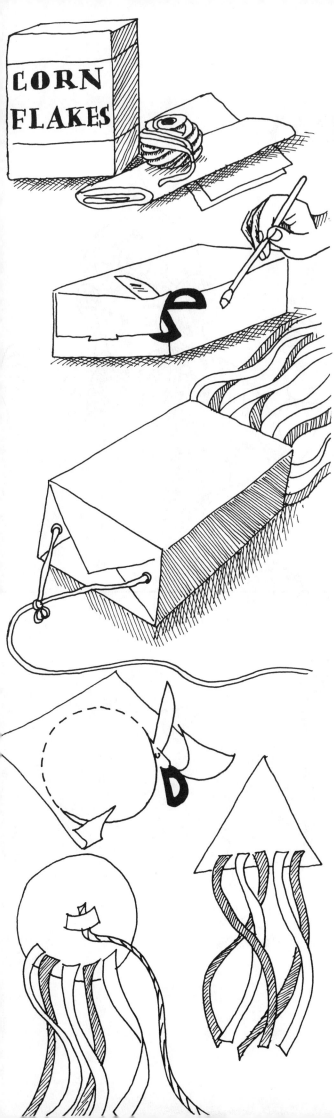

THINGS TO DO

A BOX KITE

<u>YOU WILL NEED</u>

A large cereal box, white paper, paint, string, crêpe paper, glue.

<u>METHOD</u>

1. Cut away the extra flaps from one end of the box. Cover the rest of the box with white paper, leaving one end of the box open. Paint with bright colours and allow to dry.

2. Cut the crêpe paper into long thin strips and glue them around the open end of the box.

3. Make a hole as shown and thread each hole with a long piece of string.

SMALL KITES

<u>YOU WILL NEED</u>

A4 paper, paint, string, crêpe paper, glue.

<u>METHOD</u>

1. Cut out different shapes from the A4 paper (circles, squares, and diamonds), to make small kites, and paint.

2. Cut the crêpe paper into long thin strips about 20 cm (8") long and glue them to the shapes.

3. Attach a long piece of string to one end of the small kites.

GANESA'S BIRTHDAY

September 4th

Ganesa (which in Sanskrit means, Lord of the Host) is the elephant-headed god, Siva's son. He is the Hindu god of wisdom, good fortune and the remover of obstacles.

His birthday is celebrated on the fourth day of the Hindu month Bhadrapad, which usually falls in September.

Ganesa Chaturthi is an important festival in Maharashtra, where huge clay models of him are taken out on floats. There is a great procession which includes a lot of music-making, singing, drumming, blowing of conches, (which are huge shells), and clashing of cymbals. The procession goes to the sea or to a lake and Ganesa is immersed in the water before the people return home.

HOW GANESA GOT HIS ELEPHANT HEAD

Paravati created Ganesa out of a substance, sometimes called **'mala'** (dirt) or **'lepa'** (rubbing). She rubbed it off the surface of her body and formed it into the shape of a handsome youth. Paravati commanded this young man to guard her from all intruders. When Siva came to see Paravati, the young man barred the door. During the battle that followed, Siva beheaded the youth. Paravati became angry and demanded that Siva restore him at once. So Siva sent a group of attendants (ganas) to find the first available head, which happened to belong to an elephant. Siva restored the youth with the elephant's head and gave him command over his group of ganas, and so named him Ganesa, Lord of the Group.

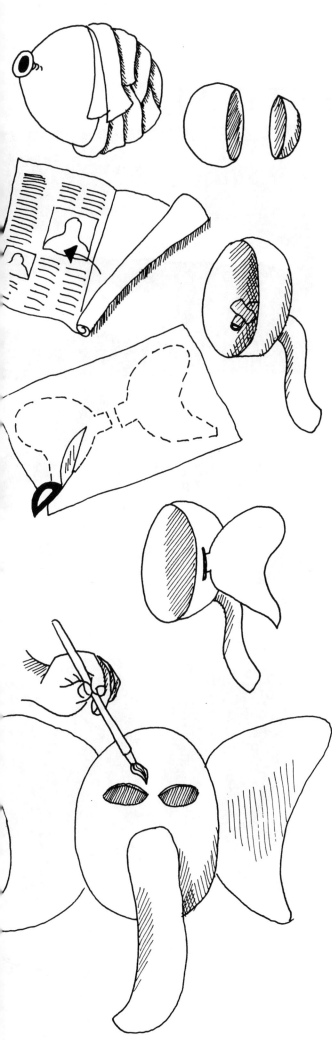

In receiving the head of the elephant, Ganesa also takes on some of the symbolism associated with the elephant in Indian culture. Elephant motifs are frequently found at the bases of temples and guarding the doors.

THINGS TO DO

AN ELEPHANT'S HEAD

<u>YOU WILL NEED</u>

Newspaper, a balloon, card, wallpaper paste, paint, sellotape, varnish.

<u>METHOD</u>

1. Cut the newspaper into strips and paste at least four layers onto the balloon. Allow to dry for several days.

2. Cut a third away from the balloon so that it can sit over the head.

3. Roll several sheets of newpaper thick enough to form a trunk. Make a hole in the front and push part of the trunk through and secure on the inside with sellotape.

4. Cut out elephant ears from the card. Make a slit either side of the balloon and slide in the ears.

5. Make two holes in the balloon for the eyes. Paint and allow to dry before giving the elephant's head a coat of varnish.

CHINESE MOON FESTIVAL

September 15th

The Chinese hold a Moon festival in September to celebrate the brightest full moon of the year. This moon-watching tradition began in the Tang dynasty (518-90). A legend about the poet Qu Yuan relates that he drowned in a pool while trying to hold the moon.

People set out in the evening to view the moon, read and write poetry and eat moon cakes.

At nightfall they greet the moon with a colourful procession of lanterns shaped like animals, birds or fish, which are made by the children. Inside each lantern is a candle because, like other autumn festivals, the Moon Festival is celebrated partly as a Festival of Lights. Since the Chinese call the moon the Queen of Heaven this is also a festival for women, when they ask the moon for good fortune in the months which follow.

Traditional foods are eaten, such as crab meat followed by fruits and little rice cakes shaped like the moon. These rice cakes are made of sesame seeds, ground lotus, dates and bean paste. They once played an important part in Chinese history. In the fourteenth century the Chinese successfully rebelled against the Mongolian rulers. They hid messages in rice cakes giving the time and place of the rebellion.

THE MOON QUEEN

This is one of the tales told around the time of the Moon Festival.

A story to read

A long time ago there lived in China a wicked king in China. Although he was a terrible person, his wife Sheung Ngao was a kind and loving woman. She was very sad at the evil her husband did.

One day the king heard of a magic potion which would make anyone who drank it live forever. He commanded his servants to search the world for the magic potion and to bring it to him.

After many adventures, the crew of one of his ships found the magic potion and brought it back to him. The king put the potion in his room and announced that, on the following day, he would drink it and by so doing would live forever. The people were very sorry to hear this, because he was such a wicked king.

Sheung Ngao realised that if the king lived forever, his people would suffer forever. So she decided to do one last act of kindness. She crept into his room that night and drank the magic potion. When the king found out, he was very angry and rushed to kill brave Sheung Ngao. But the gods lifted her from his grasp and carried her to the moon. She still lives there to this day. During the Moon Festival people look to see if they can see Sheung Ngao on the moon.

THINGS TO DO

The lanterns are of all shapes, sizes and colours - some like fish, others in various animal shapes. They form the highlight of the festival.

ANIMAL LANTERNS

YOU WILL NEED

Paper, paint.

METHOD

Fold a large piece of paper into four and cut out an animal shape as shown.

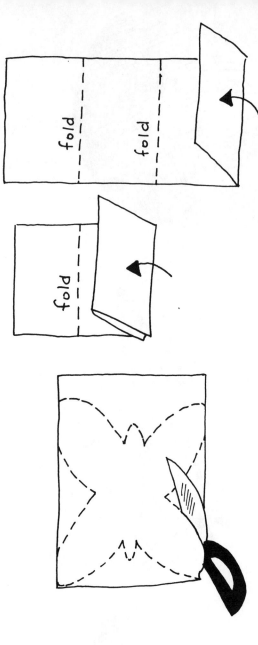

COOKING

MOON CAKES

Ideally, these cakes should be made with a Chinese moon cake mould, which imprints the correct chrysanthemum-shaped pattern and Chinese characters on the cake. Various fillings such as lotus, melon or egg, are the most common.

YOU WILL NEED

4 tablespoons brown sugar
110 g (4 oz) margarine
1 teaspoon sesame oil

4 cups flour
1/2 teaspoon salt
1 egg

For the Filling

2 tablespoons peanuts
2 tablespoons sesame seeds
2 tablespoons walnuts
2 tablespoons blanched almonds
2 tablespoons rice flour or
poppy seeds

2 tablespoons sultanas
4 tablespoons brown sugar
2 tablespoons margarine
2 tablespoons chopped
dried apricots

Oven temperature: 200' C/400' F/Gas 6

METHOD

1. Sift the flour, sugar and salt together. Cut the margarine into pieces and rub into the flour until it forms crumbs. Add enough hot water (about 1/2 cup) to make a pastry dough. Cover with a cloth.

2. Roast the peanuts in a hot pan for 2 minutes. Add the sesame seeds, putting on a lid because the seeds will jump! Roast for another 2 minutes. Put the peanuts and seeds in a grinder or mortar and grind with the other nuts. Add the rest of the filling ingredients and mix together.

3. Grease a tart tray. Roll out the pastry on a floured board. Cut rounds with a pastry cutter and place in the tray. Put in a tablespoon of filling. Press down gently. Wet the edges of the pastry and cover with another round to make a lid.

4. Beat the egg and sesame oil together and brush each cake with the mixture. This will give the tops a nice golden glaze. Bake for about 30 minutes until the cakes are a golden brown.

ROSH HASHANAH

September/Early October

Rosh Hashanah is the Jewish New Year. This two day festival usually falls in September or early October.

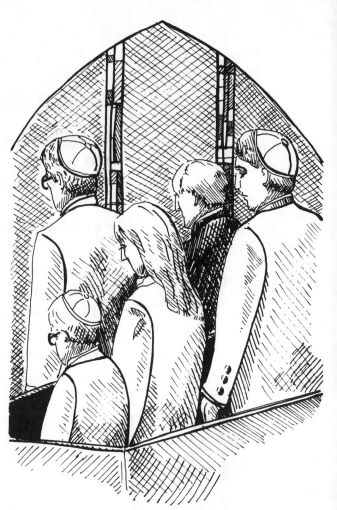

Rosh Hashanah starts a solemn period of ten days during which Jews think about the way they have behaved during the past year. According to Jewish tradition, there is a symbolic book in heaven, in which all the people's deeds are written. On one side are the good deeds and on the other, the bad deeds. The people have to examine their relationship with God and other people, and ask for forgiveness.

This is a holy time, and Jews spend much of it in the synagogue praying. They mainly wear white clothing to remind themselves of the holiness and purity of the time. A shofar (ram's horn) is sounded more than a hundred times during the two day festival.

The people celebrate God's creation of the world and remember the Bible story of Abraham. The story tells of how God commanded Abraham to take his only son Isaac, who he loved very much, and sacrifice him to God. Having great faith in God, Abraham took Isaac to a far off place, and built the altar as God had commanded. But God then decided that Isaac could sacrifice a ram instead of his son.

After prayers at the synagogue, Jewish families gather for a special meal. The table is covered with dishes using sweet foods such as raisins, carrots, and dates. Apples are eaten dipped in honey. They represent hope for a sweet and happy year ahead.

THINGS TO DO

A SHOFAR

<u>YOU WILL NEED</u>

Newspaper, a stapler, paste, grey paint.

<u>METHOD</u>

1. Take three sheets of average size news-paper. Fold each one to end up with a 2 cm (1') wide strips.

2. Roll the first strip starting with a circle 2 cm (1') in diameter. Carefully roll each strip around the other. Staple to secure every 2 cm.

3. After this is completed paste several sheets of paper around the Shofar to give a smooth finish.

4. Allow to dry and paint a light grey.

A ROSH HASHANAH CARD

There are many symbols which can be used in Rosh Hashanah cards, such as: a shofar, Kiddush (wine cup), Magen David (the Star of David), challah (bread), seasonal vegetables.

<u>YOU WILL NEED</u>

A4 card, small coloured sticky shapes

<u>METHOD</u>

1. Fold the card in half. Draw any of the symbols shown, on the card, and decorate with the shapes. Inside the card write in Hebrew "May you be inscribed for a good year" as shown.

לשנה טובה תכתבו

COOKING

Carrots are one of the few sweet-tasting vegetables and so they are very often used as a sweet vegetable dish served at Rosh Hashanah. In the USA, sweet potatoes are often used instead. There should be no sour or bitter dishes at the table, so this means that some people will not eat foods such as olives or aubergines.

CARROT CAKE

<u>YOU WILL NEED</u>

225 g (8 oz) carrots, peeled and grated
225 g (8 oz) sifted flour
110 g (4 oz) margarine
110 g (4 oz) honey
110 g (4 oz) sugar
1/2 teaspoon baking powder
1 teaspoon cinnamon
1 teaspoon nutmeg

Pre-heat the oven: 170' C/325' F/Gas 3

<u>METHOD</u>

1. Mix the flour, spices and baking powder together in a large bowl. Then melt the margarine, honey and sugar together in a saucepan. Stir this mixture into the flour, combining all ingredients thoroughly. Then stir in the carrots.

2. Put the mixture into a well greased loaf tin and bake for 60-80 minutes, until it feels firm to touch and a skewer inserted into the centre comes out clean. Leave the cake in the tin for 10 minutes before turning out.

ROUND CHALLAH

Challah is a special holiday bread which, although usually made in the shape of braid is for this holiday made round, like the snails shell. This reminds people that the year goes around and around. It is also a custom to eat sweet things such as pieces of apple dipped in honey. New fruits of the season are blessed and eaten.

YOU WILL NEED

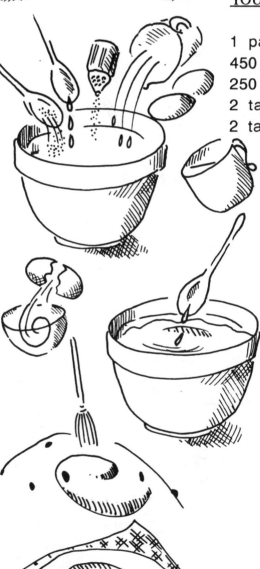

1 packet of dried yeast   6 tablespoons warm water
450 g (1 lb) plain flour   3 eggs, beaten
250 ml (8 fl oz) hot water   1/2 tablespoon salt
2 tablespoons vegetable oil
2 tablespoons sugar (or less, to taste)

Pre-heat oven temperature: 200' C/400' F/Gas 6

METHOD

1. Dissolve the yeast in the warm water and leave to ferment. Pour the hot water into a mixing bowl followed by the oil, salt, and sugar. When the sugar has dissolved and the liquid mixture has cooled to lukewarm, add the yeast, then two eggs. Mix thoroughly. Put the flour in another bowl and make a well. Then pour the liquid a little at a time into the well of the flour, to make a dough.

2. Turn out onto a floured surface and knead well. Place the dough in a greased mixing bowl, cover with a clean tea-towel for at least 2 hours until the dough has doubled in size. Knead again and form into a round shape.

3. Place on a greased and lightly-floured baking tray. Allow to rise for a further 25 minutes. Combine the yolk of the remaining egg with 1 teaspoon of cold water and mix well. Use this mixture to brush the Challah.

4. Bake 10 to 15 minutes at 200' C/400' F/Gas 6, then at 180' C/350' F/Gas 4 for 45 minutes.

LEKACH HONEY CAKE from Israel

'So David and all the house of Israel brought up the ark of the Lord with shouting, and with the sound of the horn ...... And he dealt among all the people, even among the whole multitude of Israel, both to men and women, to every one a cake of bread, and a cake made in a pan, and a sweet cake'

11 Samuel 6:15, 19

YOU WILL NEED

350 g (12 oz) self-raising flour
110 g (4 oz) caster sugar
225 g (8 oz) thin honey
1/2 level teaspoon ground ginger
1/2 level teaspoon mixed spices
1/2 level teaspoon bicarbonate of soda
10 g (1/2 oz) almonds, shredded
275 ml (1/4 pint) warm water
3 tablespoons corn oil
2 eggs

Oven temperature: 180' C/350' F/Gas 4

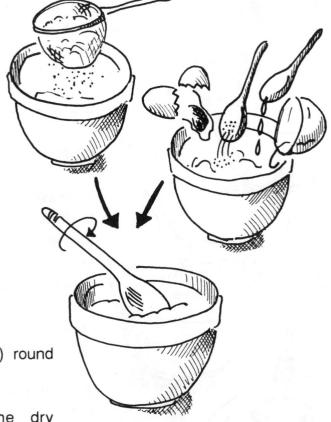

METHOD

1. Line the base and side of a 20 cm (8') round cake tin and grease well.

2. Warm the honey. Sift together the dry ingredients. Whisk together the eggs and sugar until light and creamy, then beat in the oil and honey.

3. Add the dry ingredients alternately with the liquid. Pour this batter into the prepared tin, sprinkle with almond, and bake in the centre of the oven for about 45 minutes, until well risen and firm.

YOM KIPPUR

The ten days between Rosh Hashanah and Yom Kippur are called the Days of Penitence. Yom Kippur is the day of Judgement, the most solemn and holiest day for the Jewish people, when they confess their sins and pray for forgiveness.

Having looked at the deeds of the people over the last ten days, God decides their future on the day of Yom Kippur.

The family eats before sundown on the Eve of Yom Kippur.

At the special meal on the Eve of Yom Kippur, it is traditional for most Jews to eat chicken. Chicken and rice are eaten before fasts in many countries of the world. The meal is always finished with a piece of bread and a drink of water, this is symbolic food for the fast. The fast lasts for 24 hours.

Then as the first star of evening appears in the sky, a horn is blown in the synagogue and the people hurry home to break their fast. They greet friends and relatives saying, **'May your fate be sealed for a good year!.'**

After the fast is over the family come together for a meal. It may start off with something sweet such as an apple dipped in honey. This is followed by something salty such as herring, smoked salmon, or cured salmon with soured cream.

JONAH AND THE FISH

On the afternoon of Yom Kippur, the Bible story of the Prophet Jonah is read in the synagogue.

A story to read

The Prophet Jonah heard the voice of God. It told him to go to the wicked city of Nineveh. There, he was to tell the people to change their ways or they would be punished. Jonah didn't want to do this so he ran off to the sea and boarded a fishing boat which was just setting sail.

Suddenly, far out at sea, the fishing boat was caught in a great storm. Jonah knew the storm came because God was angry with him. So he told the sailors to throw him overboard, so that the storm would end.

Jonah was thrown into the sea, and a great fish came and swallowed him up. Jonah lived in the fish's belly, where he prayed for God to forgive him. After three days, the fish spat him out on the shores of Nineveh. Although Jonah didn't want the people of Nineveh to be saved, he gave them the message from God. The people were sorry and changed their ways.

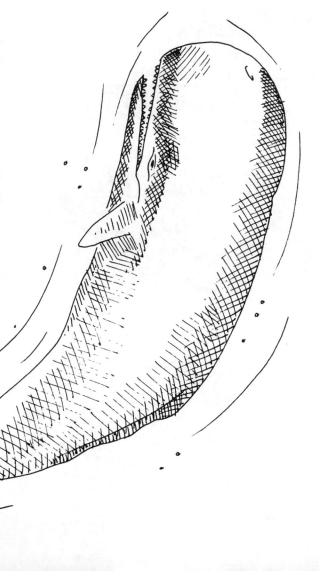

THINGS TO DO

JONAH AND THE FISH COLLAGE

<u>YOU WILL NEED</u>

A large sheet of paper, paint, cotton wool, coloured shiny paper, material, glue.

<u>METHOD</u>

1. Paint the large sheet of paper in blue. Cut out the waves as shown, paint white and allow to dry. Stick small strips of cotton wool at the edge of the waves so it looks like foam.

2. Cut out a large fish shape with its mouth wide open and decorate with the coloured shiny paper.

3. Draw and cut out Jonah and decorate him with the material.

4. Glue the fish and Jonah onto the blue piece of paper.

A SILVER KIDDUSH CUP

<u>YOU WILL NEED</u>

Three paper or plastic cups, silver foil or paper, scraps of coloured paper, glue.

<u>METHOD</u>

1. Glue the bottoms of the two cups together. Cover with silver paper.

2. Glue the scraps of coloured paper onto the cup. Put the third cup inside to hold the wine.

COOKING

ISRAELI FALAFEL

<u>YOU WILL NEED</u>

225 g (8 oz) chickpea purée 2 eggs
3-4 cloves garlic, crushed salt and pepper
4 tablespoons water plain flour and oil

Pre-heat oven: 200' C/400' F/Gas 6

<u>METHOD</u>

Mash all the ingredients together or purée in a blender to make a stiff paste. Place in the refrigerator for a few hours. Shape the mixture into balls and coat with flour. Place on an oiled, floured baking tray. Bake in the oven for 15-20 minutes until brown. Serve hot by itself, or with salad. It is commonly served in pita bread with salad, tahina (sesame paste) and harif (hot sauce).

CARROT KUGEL

<u>YOU WILL NEED</u>

50g (2 oz) potato flour or cornflour 75g (3 oz) sugar
200 g (7 oz) plain white flour 4 eggs, separated
225 g (8 oz) carrots 25g (1 oz) margarine
1 teaspoon lemon juice 1 small cooking apple
Juice and grated rind of 1 orange

Oven temperature: 190'C/375'F/Gas 5

<u>METHOD</u>

Place the egg yolks in a bowl and beat with the sugar until light and fluffy. Grate the carrot and apple finely. Squeeze out all the liquid. Mix the grated carrot, apple, orange rind, orange and lemon juice, and flour. Mix well with the egg mixture. Whisk the egg whites until stiff. Fold them into the carrot mixture. Spoon into the greased casserole. Bake for 35 minutes until golden brown.

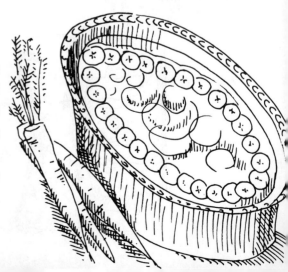

OCTOBER

'Brown October brings the pheasant;
Then to gather nuts is pleasant.'

October, like September, bears its old Roman name, which is two months out of date. It means '**the eighth month**' but it is, of course, the tenth. The Anglo-Saxons used to call it '**the yellow month**'.

OCTOBER BRINGS

October brings us Harvest things,
Vegetables, fruit, and Pearly Kings.

October brings the witch's Queen,
All on the night of Hallowe'en.

October brings the Festival of Light,
Diwali its name, and held at night.

October brings snails and spiders,
Big brown bats with wings like gliders.

October brings a shorter day,
And never enough time for us to play!

By Shirley West

HARVEST FESTIVAL

October 15th

This is usually celebrated at around 15th October when after all their hard work in the fields, the farmers gather in their crops.

In the old days, grain was cut with scythes, gathered into sheaves or bundles with sickles, then tied and left in the fields to dry. It was then taken back to the farm for threshing, when the sheaves were beaten to separate the grain from the chaff and straw.

The end of harvest was a time of celebration. Country people feasted and made merry. The last sheaf was often hung on the barn or farmhouse door for good luck until the following year.

Horses and carts used to do all the work but now the modern farmer uses a combine-harvester. They cut and thresh, collecting the grain into a big grain tank and leaving the straw behind. A pick-up bailer then gathers the straw and packs it into bundles.

CORN DOLLIES

People once believed it unlucky to cut the last of the corn in the field. They plaited the uncut stalks into a Corn Dolly and took turns throwing the sickle at it, so that everyone took part in cutting the last of the corn. Another custom was to keep the dolly till the following year and bury it in the field for luck on Plough Monday, the day on which farm workers went back to the plough after the Christmas holidays.

HARVEST THROUGHOUT THE WORLD

In Africa some countries have a Christian celebration in autumn. Others celebrate in the traditional African style with music and dance. The dancers wear masks and dance with steps and patterns that have a meaning. They tell a story and try to frighten away the spirits which they believe might spoil the harvest.

In America Thanksgiving Day falls on the fourth Thursday in November. See page 88

In Bulgaria the Queen of Grain is dressed in woman's clothes, carried around in a procession, and then burned and scattered in the fields or thrown into some water. This ritual is about the cycle of the seasons

In England, it used to be the custom to take to the church, on 1st August, Lammas Day, a loaf made from the first grain that was harvested. This loaf was used in the Eucharist (Greek for Thanksgiving) otherwise known as the Holy Communion.

In Germany and Switzerland, September is the traditional month for the shepherds and cowherds to return to the valley from the mountains. The animals are decorated with flowers, and the villagers, dressed in national costumes, turn out to welcome the shepherds home.

In Germany the Oktoberfest of Munich, on the third Sunday in October, is a special harvest festival. It celebrates the hop harvest from which the Germans make their beer. On that day there are fairs, parades and pageants.

In India at one rice festival the people get up before dawn to boil new rice. They watch eagerly, and as the first bubble rises in the pot, they cry **'Ponga! Ponga!** This is a signal that the festival has begun. Later they eat a sweet made from new rice, sugar, fruits and butter.

There is also a festival in India called **'Dusshera'** which marks the end of the rainy season and the beginning of agricultural labours. This festival ends with a ritual of the giving of alms by people carrying small fresh shoots of barley plants. Then comes **'Diwali'** marking the New Year and celebrating the sowing of winter crops.
See pages 54 and 57

In Ireland and Wales, a draught will sometimes be poured on to the earth as a compliment to the **'Good people'** or fairies.

In Israel Sukkot is a Jewish harvest festival. Festivities are held in little shelters called **'sukkahs'** built to symbolize the wanderings of the families' forefathers. The huts are decorated with harvest fruit and flowers. See page 51

In Lithuania, people dress the last sheaf of grain with ribbons and flowers, so that it looks like an old woman. They call this **'boba'** (old woman) until the next year.

In Morocco they use straw from the harvested fields and shape it into a female image dressed in clothes to represent the Bride of the Barley.

In Peru a female image is made with the biggest maize cob of the harvest. This is called the Maize Mother. They also have the Cocoa Mother, and the Potato Mother.

41

In the Punjab the cotton plant is fashioned into a female figure and is known as the Cotton Mother.

In Portugal at the '**Christian Festival of Trays**,' the people carry trays', laden with bread to church.

In Scotland there are famous Fishermen's Walk Festivals at places like Cockenzie and Musselburgh, where women dressed in the traditional dress of fisher-wives walk in procession carrying dolls' dresses in similar costumes. There is dancing in the street and an afternoon of sports and games.

PEARLY KINGS AND QUEENS

The Pearly Kings were costermongers, street vendors of fruit and vegetables. It is said their name derives from a variety of large cooking apple called costar, which was once very common.

The costumes of the Pearly Kings and Queens are said to have sprung from the arrival of a huge cargo of fashionable pearl buttons from Japan, in the 1880's. One costermonger sewed them round his wide trouser bottoms and the fashion caught on.

The Harvest Thanksgiving held by the market traders who wore these special suits began in London in 1930. They were originally approached by the Church Army who suggested the festival as a charitable exercise.

The shimmering suits, dresses and hats, handed down with hereditary titles, are sewn with mystic symbols, stars, moons, suns, flowers, diamonds, trees of life, eyes of God and fertility signs. Each outfit holds 30,000 buttons and weighs 63lbs or more. The pearly suits are worn at christenings, weddings and funerals.

Today the Pearly Kings and Queens devote much of their time to raising money for charity. Princes, Princesses, Pearly Babies and the occasional Pearly Dogs hold their annual Autumn Costers' Harvest Festival service at St Martin-in-the-Fields in London. They come bearing gifts of fruit and vegetables, which are later distributed to the needy.

The Pearly Royals arrived in Victorian times, and though some Kings and Queens still reign in their various districts, they are part of a tradition that is slowly dying.

HARVEST OF THE SEA

On the first Sunday in October, in the church of St Mary-at-Hill, Billingsgate, fish workers from the old famous London market have gathered for many years to give thanks for the **'Harvest of the Sea'**. The church is decorated with nets and equipment as well as fruit and flowers. Fish are donated by the fishmongers and after the service they are given away to old, sick or poor people. Such services are held in many seaside towns too, especially those with a local fishing fleet.

Suggested Songs: **Look at us and Watch us, Autumn is Here, Harvest in the City, Fishermen, World Harvest**, from **Festivals (all the year)**, by Jean Gilbert, published by Oxford University Press.

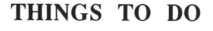

THINGS TO DO

GROW SEEDLINGS

Acorns, conkers, sycamore and ash seeds can be planted in flower pots and grown as house plants.

YOU WILL NEED

Flower pots, stones, soil, rubber band, plastic bags, sycamore seeds, chestnuts, acorns, apple or orange pips.

METHOD

1. Soak acorns or other hard nuts in warm water overnight. Peel but don't cut off the hard outer shells.

2. Put a handful of stones in the bottom of the pot, place a saucer under the pot.

3. Fill the pot two thirds full with soil or compost. Water the soil until it is moist but not soggy. Place the acorns or other seeds on top of the soil. The seeds need room to grow so plant only one seed in each pot. Cover the seed with a layer of soil.

4. Place a plastic bag over the pot and fasten with a rubber band. Place the pot in a sunny spot. As soon as the seedlings appear, remove the plastic bag. Water once or twice a week. The soil should be moist, but not wet.

5. When the seedlings has grown to several inches, dig a hole in the garden a bit bigger than the pot. Gently scoop out the seedling and the soil around it from the pot. Plant it in the hole and water it.

AN A to Z VEGETABLE AND FRUIT CHART

YOU WILL NEED

Large sheet of paper, old magazines.

METHOD

Cut out a long strip of paper. Find or draw pictures of any of the following fruit and vegetables.

avocado, asparagus, apple, apricot,
bean, brussel sprout, bamboo shoot, beetroot,
banana, blackberry,
cabbage, cucumber, carrot, cauliflower,
cherry, chestnut, coconut,
dandelion, date, damson,
eggplant, elderberry
fennel, figs,
garlic, gherkin, grape, grapefruit, greengage,
gooseberry, guava,
haricot bean, horseradish,
iceberg lettuce,
Jerusalem artichoke, jackfruit,
kidney bean, kiwi,
lettuce, leek, lemon, lime, loganberry,
mushroom, marrow, melon, mango, mint,
mulberry,
nectarine, nutmeg, nut,
okra, onion, olive, orange,
pumpkin, parsnip, pea, pepper, potato, peach,
plantain, pear, plum, pawpaw, pomegranate,
poppy seeds, peanut, parsley, passion fruit,
pineapple, quince,
radish, rhubarb, raspberry, rosemary,
seaweed, spinach, swede, strawberry, squash,
sunflower, shallot,
tomato, turnip, tamarind
ugli fruit,
vine leaves,
watercress, watermelon, walnut,

ximenia, (small tropical African plant with edible fruit, called mountain plums or wild limes,)
yam,
zucchini, zibet (a variety of chive from Asia,)

TASTE AND SMELL

Collect any of the fruits mentioned, blindfold the children and first ask them to smell the fruit and identify it. Then ask them to taste the fruit and identify it.

BREAD CLAY FOOD FOR THE SHOP

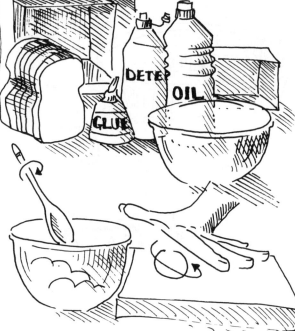

YOU WILL NEED

6 slices of bread, 1 tablespoon of white glue, 1/2 teaspoon of detergent, 1 tablespoon of cooking oil, a big bowl, paint, different size boxes.

METHOD

1. Crumble uncrusted bread into the bowl. Add the rest of the ingredients and mix until firm and not sticky.

2. Mould the dough into food for the grocery shop. For example: apples, bread, cheese, eggs, biscuits and sausages.

3. Paint the food with an even mixture of water and glue. This will stop cracks. Allow a few days to dry before painting.

4. Make the grocery stand by arranging the boxes as shown. Glue them together and paint.

5. Collect empty food packets such as cereal, soup, drink cartons. Arrange and price all the food on the grocery stand. Using play money the children can play shops.

COOKING

VEGETABLE PIE

YOU WILL NEED

1 turnip, diced and cooked
1 parsnip, diced and cooked
4 carrots, diced and cooked
110 g (4 oz) cooked peas
1 leek, washed, sliced and cooked
2 courgettes, diced and cooked

For the sauce

40 g (1 1/2 oz) margarine
2 tablespoons plain flour
4 tablespoons natural yoghurt
250 ml (8 fl oz) milk
salt and pepper

For the cheese pastry

110 g (4 oz) plain flour
110 g (4 oz) wholemeal flour
110 g (4 oz) margarine
110 g (4 oz) hard cheese, grated
2-3 tablespoons cold water
1 egg, beaten, to glaze

Oven temperature: 190 'C/375 'F/Gas 5

METHOD

1. Put the vegetables in a pie dish. Whisk all the sauce ingredients in a pan over a low heat until smooth and thickened. Pour over the vegetables.

2. Mix the flours in a bowl, then rub in the fat and stir in the cheese. Mix in enough water to bind the pastry.

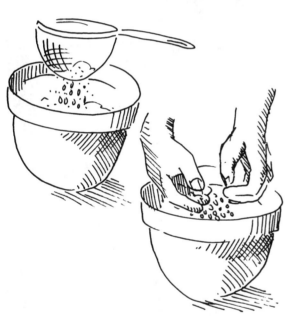

3. Roll out to a shape slightly larger than the top of the pie dish. Cover the pie, sealing the edges well. Cut the trimmings into leaf or flower shapes. Brush with the beaten egg and place the shapes to form a decoration. Brush again with the egg.

4. Bake for 40-50 minutes until golden brown.

FRUIT CRUMBLE

<u>YOU WILL NEED</u>

110 g (4 oz) flour
50 g (2 oz) margarine
75 g (3 oz) sugar
450 g (1 lb) fruit
sugar to taste
water

Oven temperature: 190 'C/375 'F/Gas 5

<u>METHOD</u>

1. Put the fruit with sugar, and very little water, into a fairly large pie dish. (Soft berries, such as raspberries and black-currants, will need no water at all). Heat in the oven for about 10-15 minutes.

2. To make the topping, sieve the flour and rub the margarine into it. Add the sugar and sprinkle the crumbs evenly over the fruit, pressing down fairly firmly.

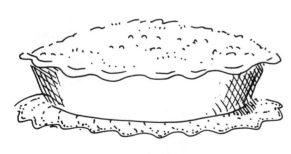

3. Bake in the oven for about 25 minutes until crisp and golden brown.

SQUIRRELS AND MICE

Squirrels and mice are both rodents. Squirrels live in trees and leap from bough to bough with extraordinary agility. Their bushy tails help them to balance as they run along the branches. Their nests, built in hollow trunks high among the branches, are called dreys. They normally have a litter of four or five at a time. Squirrels love to eat nuts, seeds of pine-cones, acorns, fruit, and sometimes birds' eggs.

Unlike most animals, squirrels can use their forepaws as hands. They also have very good eyesight and hearing. And they will always twitch their noses when they sense danger.

Grey squirrels were introduced to Britain from North America and are now more common than the Red Squirrel. They live in city parks and gardens as well as woodlands.

Mice are the smallest members of the rodent family. They eat the farmers' crops, any food they can find in houses, and even furniture and clothes! Mice don't have very good eyesight and rely on smell to find their food.

Mice usually have six families a year. There are about six baby mice in a litter. Their nests are made in any dry and sheltered spot, of rag, paper, or anything similar. Baby mice feed on their mother's milk. After about five days they start to grow fur, and by seven days their eyes open and they can hear. After about sixteen days the mother leaves them so she can build another nest for her next litter.

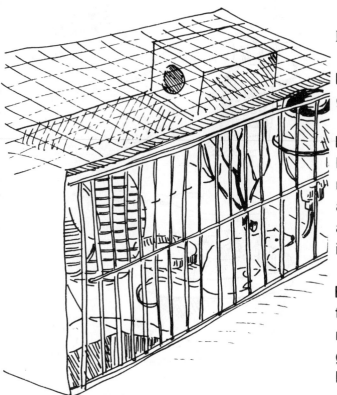

THINGS TO DO

KEEPING RODENTS AS PETS

Mice, rats, hamsters and gerbils all make good pets.

Mice and gerbils like to have company, but hamsters are used to living alone. They all need seeds and fresh greens to eat, as well as a fresh supply of drinking water. Hamsters and gerbils usually store some of their food in a special place to eat later.

Because rats and mice have very sharp teeth, their cages need to be made of very strong material. They need to have something hard to gnaw on, otherwise their teeth will grow too long.

All mice and rats like to have soft material like paper, sawdust and wood shavings for burrowing in and making nests. This also absorbs their waste, so frequent cleaning is necessary.

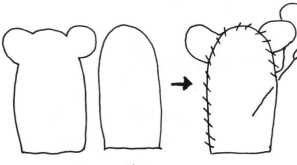

FINGER PUPPET RODENTS

<u>YOU WILL NEED</u>

Felt, cotton, wool, glue for material.

<u>METHOD</u>

1. Cut out the mouse and squirrel as shown and sew round the edge.

2. Cut out the whiskers from the wool and glue to the face. Cut out the eyes and nose as shown and glue to the rodent.

COOKING

SIX SUGAR MICE

<u>YOU WILL NEED</u>

225 g (8 oz) icing sugar
white of 1 egg
currants or silver balls
pink food colouring
thin strip of liquorice or angelica

<u>METHOD</u>

1. Sieve the icing sugar into a bowl. Whisk the egg white very lightly so that it is slightly bubbly and add 2 tablespoons of it to the icing sugar. Mix with a wooden spoon. Add a few drops of food colouring.

2. If the mixture is very dry, add a little more egg white, but the mixture must not be too damp or the mice will not hold their shape.

3. Sieve some icing sugar on to a cool surface like a plastic tray and drop a lump of mixture on to it. Lightly roll the mixture to make a short sausage shape. Pinch the sausage about 1/3 of the way along to make a neck, pinch two ears and a nose. Add two currants for eyes and a tail made from the liquorice or angelica.

SUGAR MICE

Eating sugar mice,
Is very, very nice.
Wet, sticky and gooey,
And so very chewy!
But brush your teeth that day
To wash that sugar away...

By Shirley West

SUKKOT

September/October

'On the fifteenth day of this seventh month (five days after Yom Kippur) the festival of Sukkot shall be celebrated seven days unto the Lord....'

Leviticus 23:34-36

Sukkot, also known as the Festival of Tabernacles, is a Jewish festival that marks the gathering of the Autumn harvest. The 'sukkah', which literally means 'covering' or 'shelter' is the focal point of the festival. (Sukkot is the plural form of sukkah). Historically, the Israelites travelled through the Sinai desert, camping in these temporary dwellings.

Sukkot also commemorates the time when Moses was given the Law, or Torah, on Mount Sinai.

Sukkahs are made of branches and filled with fruit. These are built in the synagogue and in home gardens.

During this eight-day festival, the first and the last two days are holy days. In modern Israel, there are special ceremonies held on the eighth day of Sukkot, when people gather at a spring, where they dance and sing songs about water. Blessings are made to God with a symbolic selection of leaves and fruit known as the Four Species. These are:

Lulav - the shoot of a young palm tree
Etrog - a citron (large lemon)
Hadas - myrtle leaves (an evergreen shrub)
Aravah - willow leaves

THINGS TO DO

MAKE A SUKKAH

YOU WILL NEED

Twigs, a large box, paint, wallpaper, string, PVA glue, cellotape, card.

METHOD

1. Remove the flaps at the front of the box leaving the back intact. Paint the outside and allow to dry.

2. Glue strips of wallpaper to the inside of the box.

3. Glue the twigs to the outside of the box covering it all over.

4. Cut out fruit shapes and paint them. Thread them on string and hang with cellotape from the ceiling of the sukkah.

FRUIT MOBILE

YOU WILL NEED

Paper plates, paint, coloured paper, glue, card.

METHOD

1. Paint the paper plates in bright colours and allow to dry.

2. Draw and cut out fruit shapes. Cut the coloured paper into small shapes and glue them to the fruit. Thread the fruit with string. Make small holes around the plate and thread the fruit on.

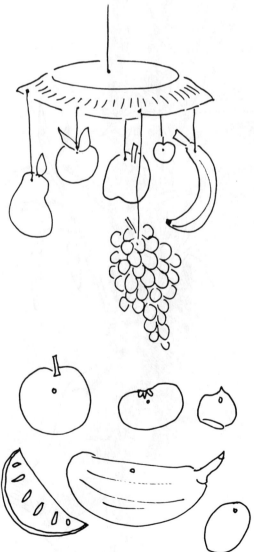

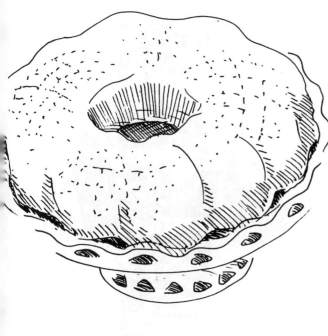

COOKING

There is no special dish served at Harvest time. The foods most likely to be on the menu would be stuffed cabbage, fried fish, strudel and honey cake.

APPLE CAKE

YOU WILL NEED

175 g (6 oz) flour
200 g (7 oz) sugar
2 teaspoons baking powder
1/2 teaspoon cinnamon
1/4 teaspoon allspice
1 egg, beaten   pinch of salt
125 ml (4 fl oz) milk
1 teaspoon vanilla essence
icing sugar and a paper doily
4 or 5 cooking apples, cut into chunks
4 tablespoons unsalted butter, melted

Oven temperature: pre-heat 180 'C/350 'F/Gas 4

METHOD

1. Grease and lightly flour a ring mould. Combine flour and salt together in one bowl. Mix the egg, milk, butter, and vanilla together in another bowl. Then add the egg mixture to the dry ingredients, and beat well.

2. Stir in approximately three quarters of the apples. Pour the mixture into the ring mould and spread evenly around the ring. Sprinkle the remaining apples evenly on top of the mixture. Bake for 30 minutes.

3. Remove from the oven and cool on a rack. Remove from the mould and decorate by placing a paper doily on top of the cake, sprinkling icing sugar on top, and then carefully removing the doily.

DUSSHERA

September/October

Dusshera is a Hindu festival which is held over ten days between the first new moon and the full moon after the autumn equinox. Dusshera literally means '**tenth day**' and is the final day of festivities. It is also known as '**Ram Lila**' and '**Durga Puja**' (nine nights).

Dusshera is a celebration of the Mother Goddess, and the triumph of good over evil. Hinduism is possibly the only religion in the world in which God is often portrayed in female form.

Dusshera is the time when the farming community waits hopefully for a good harvest. The congregational prayers always include the expression, '**Sarve Jana Sukhino Bhabautu**', which means '**Let there be happiness to all living beings**.'

At Dusshera the story of the Ramayana is told in a play, the Ram Lila, the performance of which may be spread over ten evenings. On the final night, the climax of the struggle is depicted by setting straw figures of the demon Ravana and his allies on fire with flaming arrows. The straw figures are 25 metres high and have fireworks inside them.

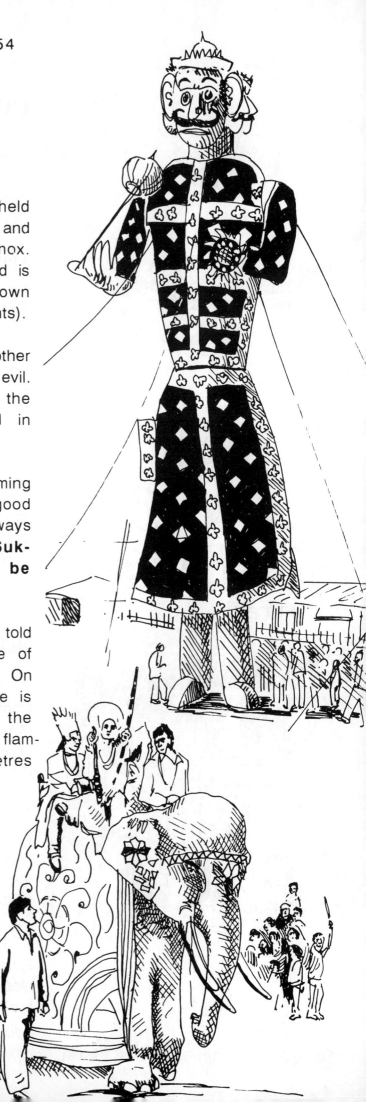

THE RAMAYANA STORY

A story to read

Once upon a time, there was a prince called Rama. A few miles away there lived a princess called Sita. Sita vowed that she would only marry the prince who could lift her father's bow, a heavy weapon. Many princes came to try their luck, but not one of them could lift the bow. Then one day Rama came along and managed to lift the bow. So Rama and Sita got married.

After the marriage, Rama's father sent him to live in the forest of Panchabuti for fourteen years. Lakshmana, Rama's brother, did not want to be parted from him, and so Rama, Sita and Lakshmana went together to the forest. They lived there happily for ten years.

Now, at that time, there lived a wicked demon king called Ravana, who had ten heads and ten arms. Ravana hated Rama and he decided to capture Sita. He changed one of his followers into a golden deer and when Sita saw the deer, she asked Rama to catch it for her. To please her, Rama went to try and catch the deer.

Then Ravana tricked Sita. He imitated Rama's voice and cried 'Help! Help!' Sita was frightened that Rama might be hurt and told Lakshmana to go to his aid. Before leaving her alone he drew a magic circle around the hut to protect her.

Then Ravana, dressed as a beggar, persuaded Sita to step out of the circle. He took her to his palace where he kept her prisoner.

When Rama and Lakshmana returned Sita was nowhere to be found. Heartbroken they set out to find her. They were helped by some monkeys including the monkey king Hanuman, and they searched all over India for Sita. They eventually found Ravana's palace and they planned a battle to free Sita.

The battle between Ravana and his demons and Rama, Hanuman and the monkeys lasted ten days.

Ravana was so strong that Rama's arrows didn't hurt him. Then the gods lent Rama a special bow and with this he killed Ravana. The battle was won and Sita was free.

On their return Rama and Sita were crowned King and Queen. Now every year Hindus celebrate the victory of Rama over the evil demon Ravana.

THINGS TO DO

RAMA LILA MASK

<u>YOU WILL NEED</u>

Card, paint, shiny paper, glue, string.

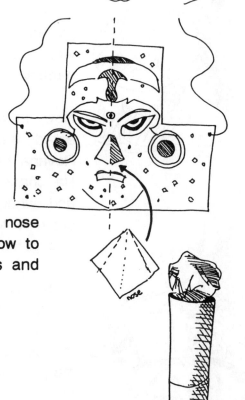

<u>METHOD</u>

Cut out the mask as shown. Cut out the nose shape and glue to the mask. Paint and allow to dry. Cut the shiny paper into small pieces and decorate the mask.

RAMA AND SITA MODELS

<u>YOU WILL NEED</u>

Two kitchen rolls, newspaper, paint, crêpe paper.

<u>METHOD</u>

1. Make two balls from the newspaper to sit on top of the kitchen rolls to form the heads.

2. Paste on several layers of torn newspaper and allow to dry for a few days. Paint and allow to dry. Decorate with the crêpe paper.

DIWALI

October/November

Twenty days after Dusshera comes Diwali, the Festival of Lights. It is celebrated by both Hindus and Sikhs during the month of October or November at the end of the rainy season, and around harvest time.

Sikhs associate this festival with the laying of the foundation stone of the Golden Temple at Amritsar by their fourth Guru, Ram Das. They also associate it with the release of Guru Hargobind from prison by the Mogul Emperor Jahangir Jains, and celebrate Diwali as the day when Lord Mahavira attained Nirvana.

Diwali (also spelt and pronounced Divali) comes from the word '**Deepavali**' meaning "cluster of lights". Small earthenware lamps called '**diwas**' are lit in every home.

A number of legends are associated with this festival. The lighting of lamps is said to invoke Lakshmi Pooja, the goddess of fortune and wealth. People believe that Lakshmi brings prosperity which is denied to those who leave their home unlit on that day. The goddess Lakshmi is worshipped at this time and her image and coins of are washed with yoghurt.

Many people settle their debts, and businesses close their accounts and open new account books in order to begin afresh on Diwali. Business people bring their books to the temple and prayers are said for a prosperous New Year.

Students worship Saraswati the goddess of Knowledge, Music and Beauty, and ask her blessing. The main religious significance of Diwali is to forgive and forget, to clear the mind of evil and reflect over the past year's events.

In preparation for Diwali, houses and shops are scrubbed clean and doorsteps are decorated with multi-coloured designs called '**Rangoli**'. Houses are painted inside and outside. New pots and pans are bought. Even the animals are washed, groomed and decorated.

People wear their best clothes or buy new ones. Very often gifts are exchanged between families and friends.

Elaborate foods are prepared, and the food most typical of Diwali is a variety of sweetmeats beautifully decorated with nuts, spices and silver paper. The silver paper used is edible. The lighting of fireworks is another essential feature of the Diwali festivities.

KALI PUJA

In Bengal, the people hold a festival in honour of Kali, the goddess of strength, disease and death.

During the festival of Kali, homes are strung with lights, and the streets are lined with shrines. The shrine is decorated with flowers and incense burners. In the centre is an image of Kali. She is shown with a fierce expression, wearing a necklace made of skulls, and with her arms uplifted. As evening falls, each shrine is lit and there is a colourful fireworks display. Finally a procession takes the images of Kali down to a river. The crowds sing, chant and ring bells as each of the images of Kali is set afloat on the water.

THINGS TO DO

DIWALI CARDS

<u>YOU WILL NEED</u>

Card, silver paper.

<u>METHOD</u>

Often these cards are made from Banyan leaves that have pictures painted on them. Decorate the outside of your card with silver paper. Write '**Sal Mubarak**' in the card - this means 'Happy New Year'.

TWO DIWAS

Diwas are small lights that are lit especially at Diwali. They are usually made of clay. Ghee (which is clarified butter or oil) is used as fuel, and cotton wool as the wick.

1. <u>YOU WILL NEED</u>

Clay or playdough, night candles.

<u>METHOD</u>

Mould the clay or playdough into a diwas shape as shown, big enough to hold a night candle.

2. <u>YOU WILL NEED</u>

Small thin candles, egg box, silver paper.

<u>METHOD</u>

Cut one section from the egg box and cover with the silver paper. Secure the thin candle to the centre with some hot wax. This must be done by an adult.

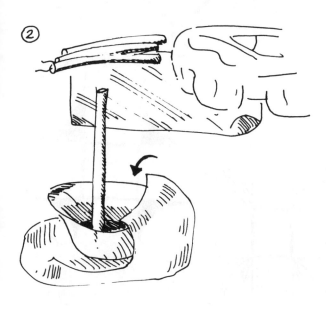

RANGOLI DESIGNS

Rangoli designs are traditionally made out of coloured sand or rice powder. They are placed outside the door of the house and are meant as a welcome sign to visitors.

A frequent design, the lotus flower, can be found drawn in many forms and usually signifies one of two things. First it can designate the human need to come to a richer understanding of mind and spirit. Just as the lotus blossom opens its petals, revealing its full beauty, so do people have this same capacity to open themselves to newer and broader levels of consciousness. Secondly, the lotus flower also appears in floor designs dedicated to Lakshmi who is known as the goddess of prosperity. The floor design is usually drawn on a pathway leading to the home and is an invitation to the goddess to enter, bringing good fortune with her.

YOU WILL NEED

Sand or rice flour, card, PVA glue, food colouring.

METHOD

1. Mix 4 tablespoons of sand or rice flour with 4 tablespoons of water coloured with food colouring. Pour off any excess liquid, then spread it out on a tray and leave to dry in a warm place. Make up several different colours.

2. Spread the glue onto the Rangoli pattern. Then sprinkle sand or rice flour onto the glue.

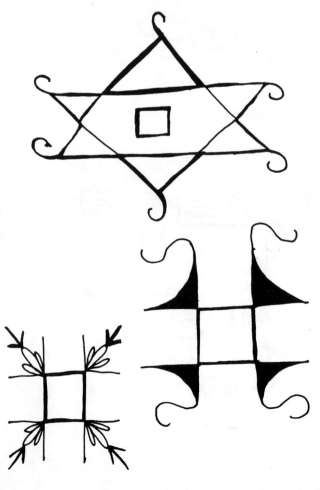

DANCE AND DRESS

Dancing plays a very important part in many festivals and celebrations. Indian dancers, regard dancing as the most beautiful of the arts. Every movement of the body, head, neck, stomach, and so on, has a particular meaning, so that whole stories can be told in mime.

This is a form of dance drama that has been used for centuries to tell the stories and legends of the Hindu gods and so help people to understand their religion. Such dancing is popular at the festival of Diwali.

HOW TO WRAP A SARI

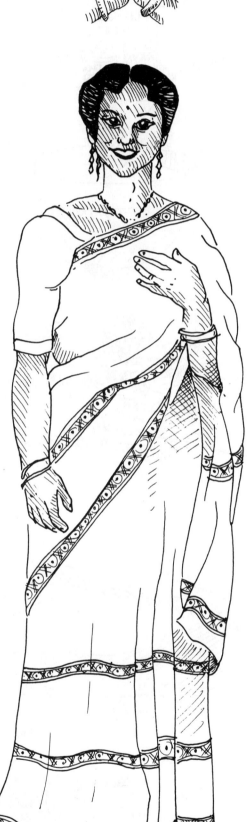

YOU WILL NEED

A large piece of material.

METHOD

1. Wrap the material around the waist to form a skirt. Then fold the loose material seven times like a fan. Make each fold about as wide as a hand.

2. Tuck the tops of the folds into the waistband checking that the hem at the bottom is even.

3. Wrap the leftover material around the body and bring up around the left shoulder. Let the long end of the sari drape down over the back. Sometimes women pull these ends over their heads to form a hood.

Suggested Songs: **Diwali**, **Hari Krishna**, from **Someone's Singing Lord**, published by A.C. Black. **The Story of Diwali in Song**, **Rama the King of Kings**, from **Festivals (all the year)**, by Jean Gilbert, published by Oxford University Press

COOKING

UNCOOKED SWEETS FOR DIWALI

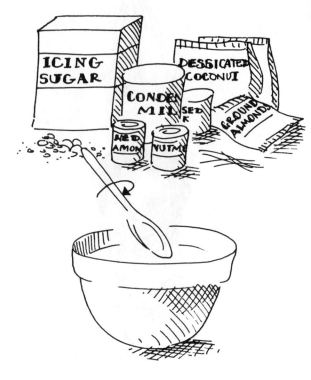

YOU WILL NEED

1 large and 1 small tin of condensed milk
2 packets of desiccated coconut
200 g (7 oz) ground almonds
1 kg (3 lb) icing sugar
110 g (4 oz) chopped nuts
a little ground cardamom
a little grated nutmeg
a few strands of saffron

METHOD

Mix all the ingredients together. Either spread the mixture in trays and cut into pieces or roll into small balls. Place in paper cases and sprinkle with icing sugar and nutmeg.

CHAPATIS

YOU WILL NEED

110 g (4 oz) wholewheat flour
4 tablespoons of water
pinch of salt

METHOD

1. Put the flour and salt in a bowl and make a well. Gradually mix in the water until a soft dough is formed.

2. Knead for 10 minutes and leave to rest for 1 hour. Divide the mixture into 6 balls. Roll into very thin rounds with a little flour.

3. Heat a tawa or heavy frying pan. Shake the flour off the chapatis and place in the pan. When bubbles appear, turn and cook the other side. Place under the grill until golden and puffy.

UNITED NATIONS DAY

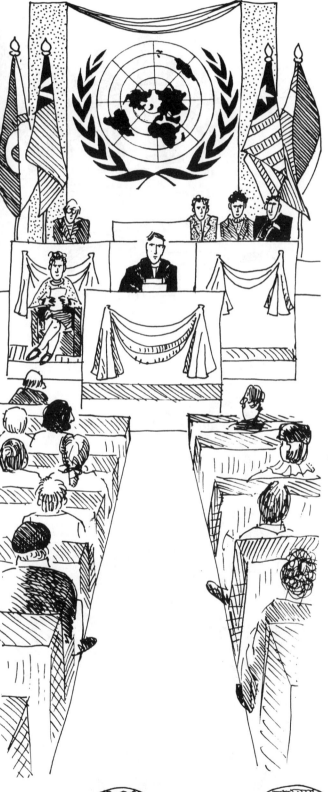

October 24th

The United Nations officially came into existence on 24th October 1945. It was formed after the devastation of the Second World War in order to maintain international peace and security. Its aims are to develop friendly relationships and to encourage co-operation between nations so that problems facing the world can be solved. There are over 149 members and the first member to join was Afghanistan in November 1946.

Most people have days called '**Red Letter Days**', this is when they remember an important happening in their history. Some are Independence Days or Liberation Days on which their country was freed.

Commonwealth Day is a reminder of the co-operation of countries throughout the world that were once the British Empire.

Europe Day celebrates the co-operation in Western Europe.

Reformation Day in Scandinavia is a reminder of Martin Luther's work, which led to the formation of Protestant churches.

Christian Aid Week focuses on the work of Christians of all denominations working together for the good of deprived people in many lands of many creeds.

western

eastern

northern

southern

ORGANIZATIONS THAT HELP

There are many organizations that have been set up in order to promote peace and harmony throughout the world.

Amnesty International was set up in 1960 as a worldwide movement independent of any government, political persuasion or religious creed. It plays a specific role in the international protection of human rights.

Greenpeace was started twenty years ago by a small group of people in Canada. Now worldwide, Greenpeace campaigns against pollution and for a cleaner environment.

Oxfam works with poor people regardless of race or religion in their struggle against hunger, disease, and poverty. Oxfam helps people in Africa, Asia, Latin America and the Middle East through relief, development, and education.

THINGS TO DO

TALK ABOUT PEACE

Symbols of peace and love are doves, hearts and flowers. There are many days set aside throughout the world which give us the opportunity to show our love for one another. For example: Mother's Day, Father's Day, Raksha Bandhan for brothers and sisters, Valentine's Day, Easter, Thanksgiving, Ch'ing Ming, Eid ul-Fitr, and Christmas.

Suggested Songs: **Magic Penny, Let there be Peace on Earth, Hévénu Shalom, Love is a Word, The Games People Play,** all from Alleluya, published by A.C. Black.

HANDS ACROSS ALL NATIONS COLLAGE

YOU WILL NEED

Paper, paint, plates.

METHOD

1. Draw an outline of the world on a large piece of paper and paint it.

2. Put some paint on flat plates. Make hand prints on the paper, allow to dry. Cut out the outline of each childs hand.

3. Draw and cut out the symbols of love: hearts, doves and flowers. Paint them and arrange these around the picture of the world.

PEACE AND LOVE CHART

Put these words on a chart:

Friends, love, hugging, stroking a pet, kissing, smiling, laughing.

Peace		
	Shalom	(Hebrew)
	Salam	(Arabic)
	Wu-Wei	(Taoist)
	Heiwa	(Japanese)
	Om	(Hindu)

THINK OF THINGS

Think of things that make you happy.
Think of things that make you smile.
Think of things that make you warm.
Think of things that make you laugh.
Think of things you like to eat.
Think of things you like to do.
Think of things you like to say.
Think of these things every day.

By Shirley West

HALLOWE'EN

October 31st

October 31st is Hallowe'en, November 1st is All Saints' Day, and November 2nd is All Souls' Day. These three days are together known as Hallow Tide. Coming a few weeks after the end of Harvest season, they mark the end of good weather and the beginning of the long winter nights.

In Celtic times, Hallowe'en marked the beginning of another year and was celebrated with the Festival of Fire. The apparently dying sun was encouraged to revive by the lighting of bonfires. It coincided, too, with the ancient Roman festival in honour of Pomana, goddess of fruits and gardens.

The lighting of fires around the villages symbolized the power of the sun, purified the empty fields and helped to keep out the witches and evil spirits. Villagers feasted and danced around the fires.

People also hung up lanterns made from turnips and pumpkins, spread salt around keyholes to keep out spies, and threw salt over their shoulders to ward off the creatures of the dark.

Masks were worn to prevent recognition by spirits which, it was thought, passed into the bodies of animals; nicknames were used for the same reason.

At Hallowe'en parties, which are generally more popular in the north of England and Scotland, chestnuts are roasted, and an omen is traced in every pop and leap. The game of **'bobbing for apples'** in a bowl of water is played.

This is the night when not only witches, but fairies, goblins and ghosts are out... The witches fly on broomsticks, or ride on the backs of cats. They go, as they did on Midsummer's Eve, to meet the devil on some high place. The devil comes to the rendezvous riding a goat. The goat carries a blazing torch between its horns to light up the revels. The Devil plays the bagpipes, and the witches dance together, making merry.

Some children in North America collect money for the Childrens' Fund of the United Nations, through UNICEF, instead of seeking treats for themselves. A favourite decoration for Hallowe'en is a Jack-o'-lantern, set in a window or on a porch. It is made of a hollowed out pumpkin with eyes, nose, and a mouth cut out so that a lighted candle inside shines through. Parties are held and children play tricks on adults who refuse to give them a treat when they knock on the door. This is known as **'Trick or Treat.'**

CATS

Many people still associate cats with the uncanny and supernatural. Unlike dogs and horses, cats are said to be fond of ghosts, and purr whenever they encounter them. Black cats are often believed to be lucky, although in Yorkshire, where it is lucky to own one, it is very unlucky to come across one by accident! White cats are usually said to bring bad luck. Witches were once said to disguise themselves as cats, and many people refused to talk near a cat, for fear that a witch would learn their secret.

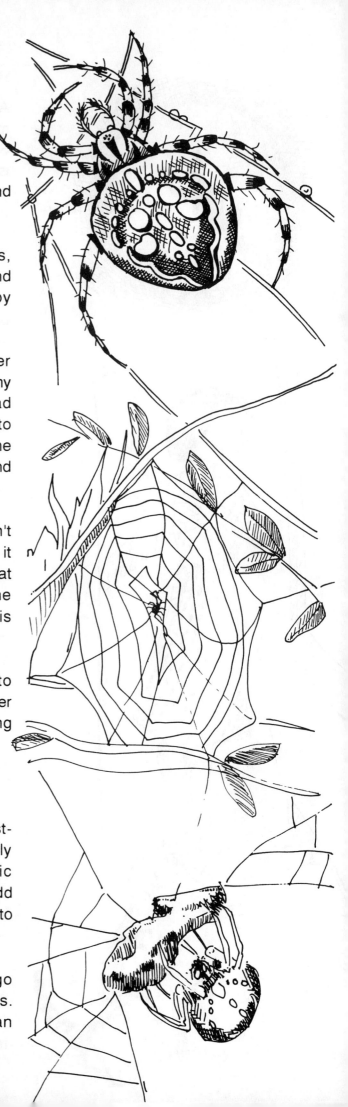

SPINDERELLA THE SPIDER

A story to read

Arachnida is the Queen of all the spiders and she has a daughter called Spinderella.

Spinderella has eight legs and eight eyes, some of which look up, some look down, and the others straight ahead. She lives all by herself in the forest.

Spinderella is always very busy spinning her web. At the end of her body, there are six tiny tubes called spinnerets which hold her thread for spinning. First she uses two of her legs to pull the thread out of her body. Then she sticks one end of the thread to a twig and starts to weave her beautiful web.

This sticky thread is very thin, so you can't see all of it. It is very strong and she uses it to catch her food. She will eat any insect that flies into her web. Spinderella wraps the insects up in her silk thread until she is ready to eat them.

Spinderella also uses her silken thread to weave a cocoon for her eggs. She carries her eggs underneath her body until the young hatch.

GUARDIAN FAIRIES

Brownies and other hobgoblins are the best-known guardian fairies: they are usually small, solitary, shaggy-haired domestic spirits, who are said to do housework and odd jobs about the home, and become attached to particular families and places.

According to tradition, most brownies go naked, or at least wear only ragged clothes. Though naturally helpful, brownies can become malicious if they are offended.

BATS

Bats are the only mammals that really fly. They are, in fact, more expert fliers than birds.

Bats are nocturnal, which means they stay awake at night. They spend the day asleep hanging upside-down in old houses and caves. Bats have fur on their bodies instead of feathers. Their wings and tails are made of leathery skin stretched across thin bones.

Many kinds of bats have good sight, but insect-eating bats have small eyes. Although these bats are not blind, their eyes are very weak. They find their way around in the dark by sending out high-pitched squeaks. These squeaks are far too high for us to hear. The sounds rebound like an echo and are received by the bats super-sensitive ears.

All young bats are born blind. They cling tightly to the underside of their mothers and grow quickly. Mother bats nurse their young with their own milk.

After about two months the young bats are ready to go out hunting by themselves. Some eat insects such as flies, gnats, beetles and moths. Others catch fish and eat fruit.

Suggested Songs: **There was an old Witch, Gobbolino the Witch's Cat,** both from **Apusskidu**, published by A.C Black. **Witch Witch, Hallowe'en,** from **Festivals (all the year)**, by Jean Gilbert, published by Oxford University Press. **Jack-O-Lantern**, from **A Musical Calendar of Festivals**, published by Ward Lock Educational. **Pumpkin Pie Song, from Festival Family and Food**, by Diane and Judy Large, published by Hawthorn Press. **Spiders and Creepy Crawlies**, from **Knock at the Door**, by Jan Betts, published by Ward Lock Educational.

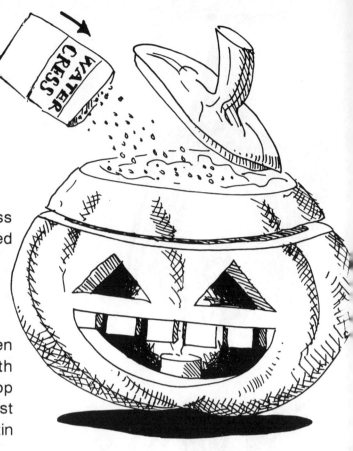

THINGS TO DO

A PUMPKIN LANTERN WITH HAIR

YOU WILL NEED

A pumpkin, night candle, tissues, water cress seeds. Marrows or melons could be used instead of a pumpkin.

METHOD

1. Slice the top off the pumpkin, and then slice a little off the top. Fill the top with wet tissues and sprinkle on the seeds. Scoop out the pumpkin flesh and seeds from the rest of the pumpkin. (See page 72 for Pumpkin Pie)

2. Cut a face out as shown. Place a candle on a saucer and put it inside the pumpkin or use a night candle.

WHAT TO DO WITH THE SEEDS

1. Wash the seeds from the pumpkin. The seed can be used to make a necklace or pip collage.

2. Try growing the seeds by drying them first, then sow in a good compost and water well.

WALL FRIEZE

Pumpkins - orange paper stuck on a pumpkin shape, yellow triangles for the eyes etc. Round plates for **cats masks** - make a cotton wool nose, use wool for whiskers. For **ghosts** - white sponge painting with black circles for eyes. Make **spiders** from egg cartons and black pipe-cleaners.

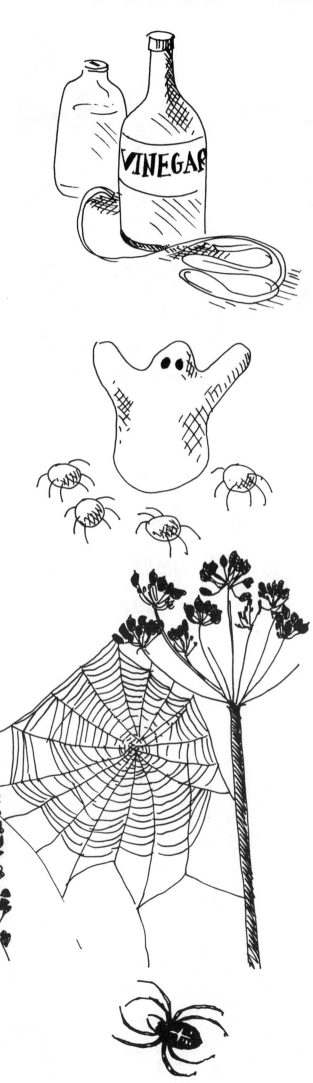

PLASTIC GHOSTS AND SPIDERS

YOU WILL NEED

1/2 cup (5 fl oz/150 ml) of milk, 4 teaspoons of vinegar, shearing elastic.

METHOD

1. Simmer the milk and vinegar in a saucepan. (The milk will curdle if you over-boil it).

2. The liquid will become a rubbery blob. Wash in cold water. Mould some into ghost shapes and the rest into spiders. Make a hole in the mixture. Allow to harden for 24 hours before threading with shearing elastic.

PRESERVING A SPIDER'S WEB

Find a good web and spray it carefully with an ozone friendly white paint. Paint a thin layer of glue onto a sheet of black card and bring it up close to the web. Press onto the web. Cut the supporting threads and finish off with a protective layer of ozone-friendly spray varnish. Don't worry - the spider will soon make another web!

PARTY GAMES

Bobbing for apples: Float apples in a bowl of water. The children have to keep their hands behind their backs and try and take a bite out of an apple. Hang apples or doughnuts from the ceiling with string and the children have to try and take a bite out of them.

Ghost and witch costumes can be made from old white or black sheets.

Hunt the spiders: Cut out lots of little spider shapes from black paper and hide them round the room. Each child can count how many spiders they have found!

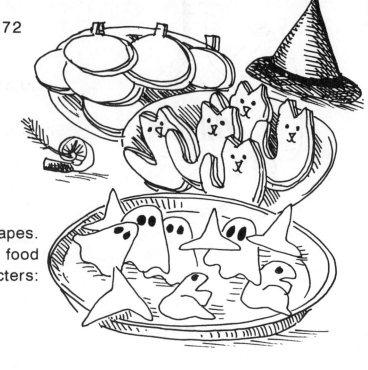

COOKING

A HALLOWE'EN PARTY

Party food

Sandwiches cut into pumpkin or cat shapes. Cakes or biscuits baked with green food colouring and cut into hallowe'en characters: ghosts, spiders, frogs, cats, witches.

PUMPKIN PIE

Pumpkin bread and stew can also be made.

<u>YOU WILL NEED</u>

1 1/2 cups pumpkin pulp	1 cup castor sugar
1/2 teaspoon salt	3 eggs, separated
1 tablespoon gelatine	1/2 cups milk
crushed mixed nuts	baked pie case
1/2 teaspoon ginger	whipped cream
1/2 teaspoon nutmeg	
1/2 teaspoon cinnamon	

Oven temperature: 190 'C/375 'F/Gas 5

<u>METHOD</u>

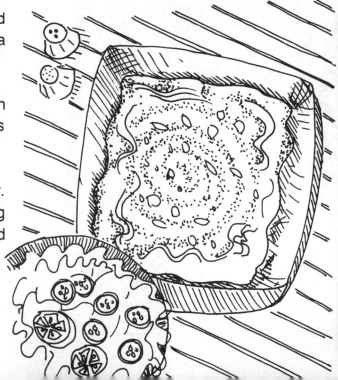

1. Beat egg yolks with 1/2 cup sugar. Add pumpkin, milk and seasonings. Cook in a saucepan, stirring until it thickens.

2. Add gelatine which has been soaked in water for 5 minutes. Stir until gelatine is dissolved and cool.

3. Beat egg whites stiff with 1/2 cup sugar. When gelatine begins to thicken, fold in egg whites and sugar, pour into pie case and garnish with whipped cream and mixed nuts.

WITCHES NIGHT

Tonight's the night when witches fly,
On their broomsticks in the sky.
Spiders and bats and cats do cry,
Watching the witches passing by.

Out in the dark and cold of night
Ready and waiting to give you a fright.
Witches screaming in the moonlight,
Waiting, silently for their flight.

They fly over hills and far away
To the land they call The Witch's Way.
Here they rest and sleep all day,
And come back at night to find their prey.

By Shirley West

UGLY WITCH

Oh ugly witch what do you eat?
'Lizards, toads, and bats so sweet.'

Oh ugly witch where do you fly?
'Over the roofs and under the sky.'

Oh ugly witch where is your home?
'In The Witch's Way shaped like a dome.'

Oh ugly witch when can you be seen?
'On the witch's night called Hallowe'en!

By Shirley West

WHAT AM I?

They chose me for my brother,
'That's the nicest one', they said.
And they carved me out a face,
And put a candle in my head.

And they set me on the doorstep,
Oh the night was dark and wild.
But when they lit the candle,
Then I smiled.

Answer: A Hallowe'en pumpkin.

By Dorothy Aldis

THE MAKING OF A CHARM

Round about the cauldron go:
In the poisoned entrails throw.
Toad, that under cold stone
Days and nights has thirty-one
Sweltered venom sleeping got
Boil thou first i' th' charmed pot!

Double, double toil and trouble:
Fire burn and cauldron bubble.
Fillet of a fenny snake,
In the cauldron boil and bake:
Eye of newt and toe of frog,
Wool of bat and tongue of dog,
Adder's fork and blind-worm's sting,
Lizard's leg and howlet's wing.
From a charm of powerful trouble,
Like a hell-broth boil and bubble.

Double, double toil and trouble:
Fire burn and cauldron bubble.
Cool it with a baboon's blood,
Then the charm is firm and good.

By William Shakespeare,
from Macbeth Act IV Scene 1

NOVEMBER

'Dull November brings the blast-
Hark! the leaves are whirling fast.'

November is the eleventh month in our calendar, but means 'ninth' month - it is another name from the old calendar which has not been altered, though its place in the year has been moved. To our Anglo-Saxon ancestors, November was '**Blotmonath**,' or '**Blood Month**', when they killed off the animals they could not feed during winter

AUTUMN FIRES

Many bonfire nights held in various parts of the country have roots which go back to days long before the Christian era. This was when the fire was used as part of seasonal celebrations to help welcome the sun.

The ancient Celtic peoples of Britain had a festival called 'Samhain' (Summer end), which fell at the end of October. The sun was then becoming weaker and it was believed that huge bonfires would help the sun to keep its strength.

Part of the celebration included singing and dancing round the fire as an offering to the gods. The Navaho Indians of North America, for example, have a ritual fire dance in which the men, with white painted bodies, dance around very close to the fire, sometimes leaping as high as the flames themselves.

Sometimes, fire festivals were associated with fertility and the next year's harvest. An old superstition said that one should jump over the dying embers and next year's crop would grow as high as one jumped.

As soon as the corn harvest is over, the ground is prepared for the next year's crop. Unburned stubble is ploughed up. Sometimes an extra crop of grass called a 'catch' crop is sown. This can be harvested in November or left for spring grazing.

ALL SOULS' DAY

November 2nd

November 2nd is by tradition the Day of All Souls, when it was believed that the unhappy souls of the dead would return to their former homes.

The festival was first kept nearly a thousand years ago. A shipwrecked pilgrim was told by a hermit that the souls of the dead who had not yet gone to heaven were crying out because people were not praying enough for them. The pilgrim told the Abbot of Cluny, who set aside the day after All Saints' Day as All Souls' Day.

Almost all religious people believe that when a person dies, a part of them which is usually called the soul continues to live in another place. Hindus, Buddhists and Sikhs believe that people are reincarnated. This means that the soul returns to earth many times as a new person before it finally goes to heaven. Jews, Christians and Muslims believe you can only live once. When you die, God will decide if you have been a good or bad person and whether you will go to heaven or be punished.

Teachings about reincarnation are read from the Hindu holy books:

'It is certain the people die, and it is certain that after death people are born again, so, do not be sad about what will certainly happen. As a person leaves old clothes and puts on new ones, so the Spirit leaves one body and enters a new one.'

In the Andes everyone must look their best. Necklaces are worn and they are very important. No Indian girl will be seen in public without one. They believe that people's souls are hungry so they take potato, corn and biscuits to offer to the dead.

In China the festival '**Yue Lan**,' or the '**Festival of the Hungry Ghosts**', is celebrated. It was believed that, on that day in summer, ghosts were released to roam around the world for one day. So, to help them on their journey, roadside fires were kindled where paper money, fruits and other offerings could be offered to the ghosts.

In Ghana the Ashanti people have a special ceremony known as '**Adae**', when their ancestors are remembered. Stools represent the ancestors and food and drink are placed in front of them. They ask their ancestors to speak to the gods, asking them for health and good fortune.

In Mexico, marigolds are placed on the graves and large groups of masked dancers can be seen.

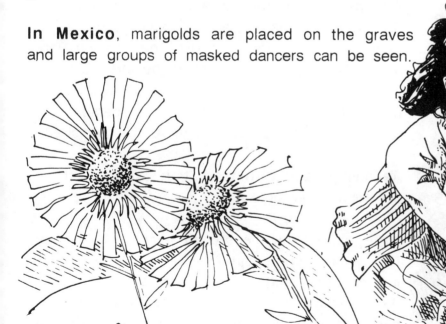

Suggested Songs: **Souling Song**, from **Festivals (all the year)**, by Jean Gilbert, published by Oxford University Press. **Soul Cake Song**, from **Festival of Family Food and Friends**, by Diane and Judy Large, published by Hawthorn Press.

COOKING

Some people believed that, on All Souls' Day, the souls of the dead actually came to visit their old homes, and so they made special 'Soul Cakes' from a light dough.

In the Andes, pastry babies are baked as an offering to the mountain gods. These are like gingerbread men but not as flat.

SOUL-CAKE

YOU WILL NEED

450 g (1 lb) plain flour
175 g (6 oz) caster sugar
175 g (6 oz) margarine
75 g (3 oz) currants
1 teaspoon ground mixed spice
3 egg yolks
a little milk, to mix

Oven temperature: 180 'C/350 'F/Gas 4

METHOD

1. Cream the margarine and sugar together in a bowl then beat in the egg yolks, one at a time.

2. Sift the flour and spice into another bowl then add to the margarine mixture. Stir in the currants, and add the milk if necessary to form a soft dough.

3. Form the dough into flat cakes and mark each with a cross. Put onto a greased baking tray and bake for 10-15 minutes until golden brown.

GUY FAWKES

November 5th

WHO WAS GUY FAWKES?

Guy Fawkes, or Guido, was born at York on April 16th, 1570. His parents were both Protestants. But his stepfather, if not a Roman Catholic himself, was connected with many great families belonging to that faith, and Guy soon became a convert.

Catholics were not popular in the seventeenth century because they disagreed with the teachings of the Church of England and they wanted a Catholic King.

In 1605, a group of Catholics with very strong feelings decided that they not only wanted to worship in their own way, they also wanted everyone else to join the Catholic church. They felt that the only way to achieve this would be to get rid of the King and Parliament.

Guy Fawkes and a group of conspirators bought the house next to the House of Lords and started to dig a tunnel. This took nearly a year to build. They bought thirty-six barrels of gunpowder and stored it in a cellar directly under the House of Lords.

Guy Fawkes had served for some years in the Spanish armies in Flanders, and he had a good knowledge of explosives.

The plan was for Guy Fawkes to set the fuse when the King and his son came to attend the opening of Parliament. However, the plan went wrong when one of the plotters wrote to his brother-in-law warning him not to attend the opening.

Guy Fawkes and the seven other plotters were found guilty of treason and executed.

Parliament decided that, since the plot had been discovered and no-one had been hurt, November 5th should be a public holiday.

Today it is no longer a public holiday, but children still make up figures to represent Guy Fawkes. And they still ask for a '**penny for the Guy**.' The Guy is then burnt on the 5th of November bonfire.

'Please to remember
The fifth of November,
Gunpowder treason and plot;
I know no reason
Why gunpowder treason
Should ever be forgot.'

Although bonfires are now linked with November 5th, these activities may have evolved from fires which were lit during the Celtic Festival of Samain on November 1st. This was when fires were lit to ensure the sun's return after the winter. Samain became All Saints' Day and among both pagans and Christians, November was associated with the cult of the dead.

Suggested Songs: **Picking up Conkers**, from **Festivals (all the year)**, by Jean Gilbert, published by Oxford University Press. **Guy Fawkes**, from **A Musical Calendar of Festivals**, published by Ward Lock Educational.

THINGS TO DO

Bonfire Night can be a time for traditional autumn games like **Conkers.** Conkers are the nuts of the horse chestnut tree. To make conkers stronger, soak them in vinegar or in salt water and bake them in the oven for about half an hour.

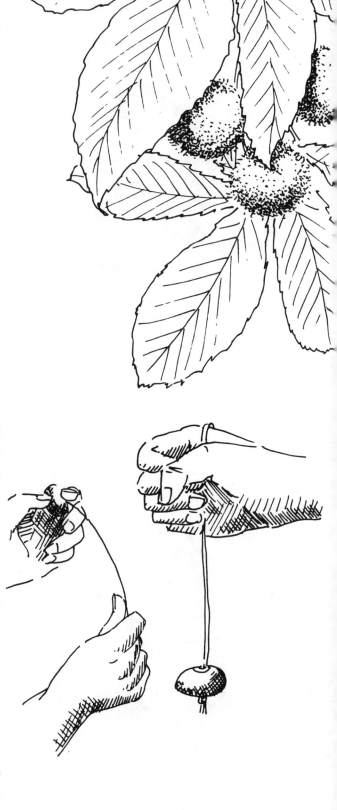

HOW TO PLAY CONKERS

YOU WILL NEED

2 conkers, string.

METHOD

1. Make a hole through each conker and thread the string. The string should be long enough to wrap twice round the hand and then hang down 23 cm (9").

2. Player 1 allows their conker to dangle by the string. Player 2 holds their conker in one hand and the end of the string in the other. Player 2 draws back the conker and tries to strike Player 1's conker.

3. Player 1 is allowed three attempts to make a hit. If the string gets tangled up, the player is allowed to shout 'strings' and claim an extra shot.

4. Player 2 then has a chance to strike and the game continues until one or other conker is destroyed.

FIREWORK COLLAGE

Remind the children about the dangers of fireworks: You mustn't play with fireworks. Don't put them in your pocket. An adult should always be present. If you see a used firework on the ground don't pick it up. Stand well back and don't throw fireworks.

YOU WILL NEED

Kitchen and toilet rolls, large sheet of paper, red crêpe paper, paint, shiny paper, twigs, leaves, white paper, glitter, glue.

METHOD

1. Models of fireworks can be made from kitchen and toilet rolls. Decorate the rolls with the shiny paper. Cut the crêpe paper into long thin strips and glue to one end of the roll to represent the flames.

2. Paint the top half of the large sheet of paper dark blue and the bottom half dark green. Allow to dry.

3. Glue the twigs to the large sheet of paper to form a bonfire. Place small strips of the red crêpe paper between the twigs for the flames. Glue the leaves along the bottom of the picture.

4. Cut out star shapes from the white paper. Glue and sprinkle with glitter. Glue the stars and the rockets to the sky.

5. Cut out children and adult shapes and paint and decorate. Allow to dry before placing on the collage.

COOKING

BONFIRE POTATOES AND CHESTNUTS

YOU WILL NEED

 large baking potatoes
450 g (1 lb) chestnuts

Oven temperature: 220' C/425' F/Gas 7

METHOD

1. Scrub the potatoes, and slit them along the top with a knife.

2. Slit the domed surface of the chestnuts with a knife and place on a baking tray.

3. Place both the potatoes and the chestnuts in the oven. Bake the chestnuts for 10-15 minutes.

4. Bake the potatoes for about an hour depending on their size.

5. Finish them off on the bonfire. Peel the chestnuts while they are still hot.

6. To fill the potatoes, enlarge the slit in the top of the potato and make another cut at right angles to it. Fill with your favourite filling.

A STUFFED LITTLE GUY

Here sit I,
A stuffed little Guy,
With my legs in the bonfire,
And my head in the sky.

Burning away,
On Guy Fawkes Day,
With my fire a glowing
When the wind is blowing.

Never having a good time,
While adults drink wine.
I'm just stuck on this heap,
Ready to weep.

A mask for my face,
Head hung in disgrace.
And straw for my hat,
And my feet are flat.

It won't be very long,
Before all my body's gone.
Then suddenly in a flash,
I become nothing but ash.

By Shirley West

REMEMBRANCE DAY

November 11th

'In Flanders fields the poppies grow
Between the crosses, row on row
That mark our place: and in the sky
The larks, still bravely singing, fly,
Scarce heard amid the guns below.'

By John McCrae 1915

At 11.00 a.m. on November 11th 1918, the guns stopped firing after the four years of World War 1.

On Remembrance Day in Britain, Queen Elizabeth attends a service at the Cenotaph in Whitehall, London. She and others lay wreaths in memory of those who died.

Poppies are used in the remembrance wreaths everywhere because they grew in the French fields of Flanders, where the men of World War 1 fought. They are also a reminder of the red blood that was lost in fighting. The money raised by selling poppies helps care for people who suffer in wars.

THINGS TO DO

MAKING POPPIES

<u>YOU WILL NEED</u>

Paper, poppies, alcohol, poppy seeds, glue.

<u>METHOD</u>

Soak the petals of the poppy in some hot water with a little alcohol and soon the water will turn into red ink. Cut out two petals as shown and paint with the red ink. Cut out a small circle for the centre of the flower and glue poppy seeds on. Glue each petal on top of each other in the middle. Roll a piece of paper to form the stem and staple to the poppy head.

COOKING

BLUE POPPY SEED CAKE

The seeds from the poppy yield oil used in making paint and cheaper grades of salad oil. They are used in some countries for decorating bread, but they can also be used in sweet pastry fillings and cakes.

<u>YOU WILL NEED</u>

225 g (8 oz) plain wheatmeal flour
225 g (8 oz) margarine
225 g (8 oz) light raw cane sugar
110 g (4 oz) blue poppy seeds
225 ml (8 fl oz) milk
3 eggs, separated
1 1/4 teaspoons baking powder

Oven temperature pre-heated 180' C/350' F/Gas 4

<u>METHOD</u>

1. Line and grease a 20.5cm (8') cake tin. Bring the poppy seeds to the boil in the milk, then turn off the heat and let them soak for 25 minutes in a covered pan.

2. Cream the margarine and sugar together until light and fluffy. Add the egg yolks, one at a time, and beat them thoroughly.

3. Mix the flour and baking powder together and fold this into the creamed mixture. Then stir in the soaked poppy seeds and milk.

4. Whisk the egg whites until they are stiff and fold them in carefully. Spoon the mixture into the cake tin and bake for 1 hour or until the centre feels firm and a skewer inserted into the cake comes out clean. Let the cake stand in the tin for 10 minutes, then turn it out onto a cooling rack.

THANKSGIVING

Fourth Thursday in November

Although this is an American holiday, it has roots in Britain.

In 1620, a group of English and Dutch families sailed from Plymouth to North America in the ship the '**Mayflower**.' They thought they would find peace and freedom from their own church. These people are now remembered as the '**Pilgrim Fathers**.' Conditions were very bad and many of the settlers died. The local Indians were friendly and showed the Pilgrim Fathers how to grow the local crops of sweet potatoes, sweetcorn and pumpkin. They also showed them how to catch and breed wild turkey.

The Governor, William Bradford, was so relieved to see the harvest gathered with the help of the Indians that he ordered a three-day festival. An invitation was sent to the local Indians to share in their celebrations. They brought turkeys and venison to add to the ducks, geese and fish provided by the settlers.

Gradually, Thanksgiving Day spread throughout New England. It was President Lincoln in 1863 who proclaimed that the day should be observed throughout the United States.

In Canada it is observed on the second Monday in October.

Suggested Songs: **Battle Hymn of the Republic**, from **A Musical Calendar of Festivals**, published by Ward Lock Educational.

THINGS TO DO

GROWING PEANUTS

<u>YOU WILL NEED</u>

Peanuts, compost, flower pots.

<u>METHOD</u>

1. Crack the shells of the peanuts and plant them still in their shells in wet compost.

2. After five days or so the roots will start to grow down, pushing the shell upwards out of the earth.

3. A week later green leaves will sprout.

A TURKEY PICTURE

<u>YOU WILL NEED</u>

Paper, paint, crêpe paper, glue

<u>METHOD</u>

1. Cut a circle 30 cm (1 ft) and 8 cm (3') in diameter.

2. Make lots of hand prints with paint and cut them out. Arrange 4 or 5 round the circle as shown. Then arrange another row behind them to form the turkey's feathers.

3. Cut oval shapes from the crêpe paper and glue them to the turkey as shown.

4. Glue the smaller circle in the middle of the bigger circle and draw a beak and eyes.

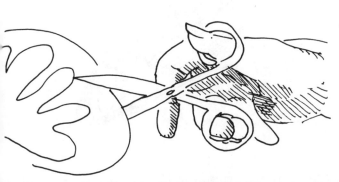

5. Cut out two claws and glue them to the turkey's body.

COOKING

CANDIED SWEET POTATOES

This is one of the traditional Thanksgiving side dishes and is served with roast turkey or roast chicken.

<u>YOU WILL NEED</u>

700 g (1 1/2 lb) sweet potatoes
75 g (3 oz) brown sugar
10 g (1/2 oz) margarine
a little grated lemon rind
1 tablespoon lemon juice

Oven temperature: Pre-heat 190' C/375' F/Gas 5

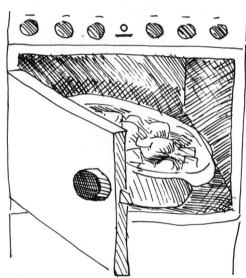

1. Peel and dice the sweet potatoes and boil in a saucepan for 8-10 minutes until the potatoes are tender.

2. Drain well and spoon into a casserole dish.

3. Mix the sugar with the lemon rind and lemon juice, and spread this mixture over the top of the potatoes.

4. Dot the top with the margarine and bake for 35 minutes.

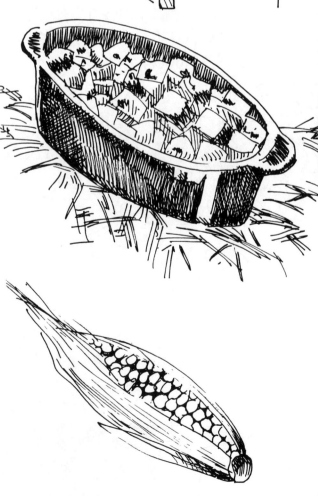

SHICHI-GO-SAN

November 15th

Shichi-go-san is a very old festival held in Japan. Shichi-go-san, in Japanese, literally means seven-five-three.

On this day, children dress in their best clothes. Most will follow the old customs and wear their traditional kimonos. These are brightly coloured robes made of cotton or silk. Each child has a long, narrow paper bag decorated with a pine tree, a tortoise, and a crane. These are symbols of youth and long life.

Parents take their children, girls aged seven, boys aged five and all children at the age of three, to the temple. There they express their happiness that their children have reached their ages and pray for their future health and happiness.

Outside the temple there are stalls where the parents buy long sticks of red and white candy known as '**candy of a thousand years**' and toys to fill the children's paper bags.

ST ANDREW'S DAY

November 30th

St Andrew was a fisherman and was one of the twelve disciples of Jesus. He was the brother of St Peter, and had previously been a disciple of John the Baptist.

By trade he was a fisherman on the Sea of Galilee. After meeting Jesus he gave up fishing to follow Jesus. After Jesus' death he was taken prisoner for being a Christian and condemned to death by crucifixion. Legend has it that he acknowledged that he was not worthy to die as Jesus had died and so elected to be crucified on a diagonal cross. This has become known as St Andrew's cross. In the Scottish flag it is white (for his purity) on a blue background (for the sea which he loved).

The name Andrew in Greek means '**manly**' and this is sometimes associated with the bravery of the Scottish people, in times of danger.

There are many legends about the manner in which the relics of St Andrew came to rest in Scotland. It is said that a group of monks set out from Constantinople (now Istanbul) to reach Scotland with the good news of Jesus and to convert the Scottish people to Christianity. They asked for the relics of some holy man to take with them as a protection from all the dangers of the voyage. They were given the relics of St Andrew and after many months of travel they arrived in Scotland. There they buried the relics and set up an altar within a small church on that spot. They called this settlement St Andrew's.

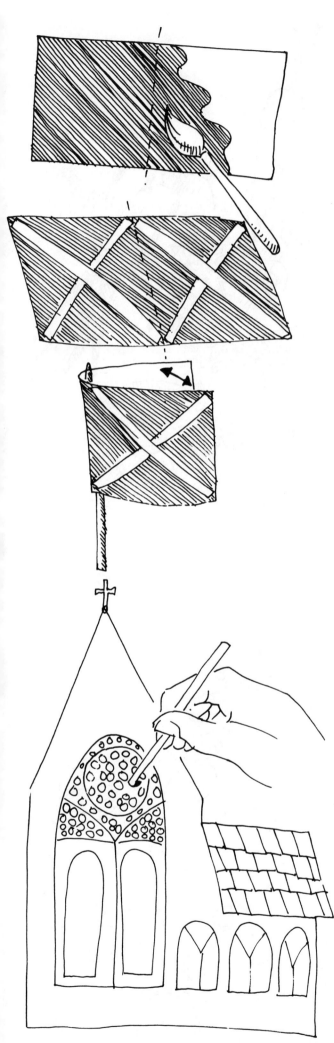

THINGS TO DO

ST ANDREW'S FLAG

YOU WILL NEED

White paper, blue paint, thin stick

METHOD

1. Cut the paper into a flag shape, paint blue and allow to dry.

2. Cut some white paper into long strips and glue to form the white cross as shown.

3. Attach the flag to the stick.

ST ANDREW'S CHURCH

YOU WILL NEED

Large sheet of paper, thick paint, glue, straws.

METHOD

1. Cut the paper into the shape of a church, paint grey and allow to dry. Paint another large sheet of paper in brown and when it is dry cut into small oblong shapes to form the tiles for the roof. Cut out a door shape.

2. Cut out 4 glass windows as shown. Place some different coloured paints in separate dishes. Dip the tip of the straw into the paint and press lightly on the window. Repeat this with the other colours until the window is covered. Allow to dry before gluing to the church.

3. Glue the tiles and door onto the church.

COOKING

In Scotland, oats and barley have always been the staple grains, and porridge is a traditional breakfast.

SCOTCH BROTH

YOU WILL NEED

700 g (1 1/2 lb) shin of beef, cut into pieces
1 medium carrot, peeled and chopped
1 medium turnip, peeled and chopped
1 medium onion, skinned and chopped
2 medium leeks, trimmed, chopped and washed
45 ml (3 tablespoons) pearl barley
chopped fresh parsley, to garnish
salt and pepper

METHOD

1. Put the meat into a saucepan, cover with 2.3 litres (4 pints) water, season to taste and bring to the boil. Cover and simmer for 1 1/2 hours.

2. Add the vegetables and barley. Continue to simmer, covered, for a further hour or until the vegetables and barley are soft. Skim off any fat and serve, garnished with chopped parsley.

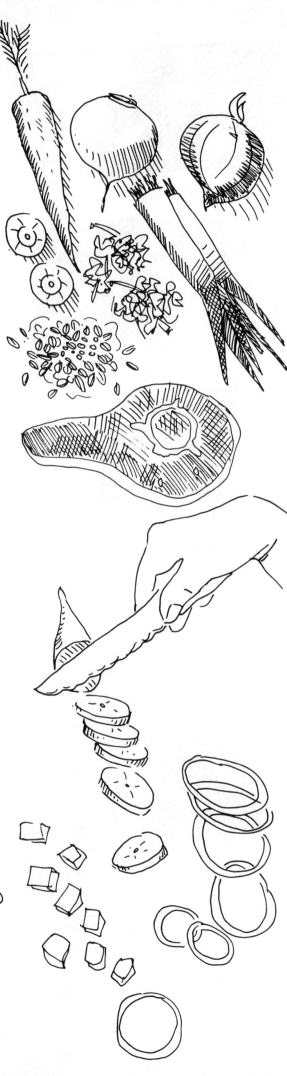

PETTICOAT TAILS

These are traditional Scottish shortbread biscuits that date back beyond the 12th century. The triangles fit together into a circle and are the same shape as the pieces of fabric used to make a full-gored petticoat in the Elizabethan times. The biscuits got their name because in those days the word for a pattern was a **'tally'**, and so the biscuits became known as '**petticote tallis**'.

YOU WILL NEED

110 g (4 oz) butter, softened
150 g (5 oz) plain white flour
50 g (2 oz) caster sugar, plus extra for dredging
50 g (2 oz) ground rice

Oven temperature: 170 'C/325 'F/Gas 3

METHOD

1. Cream the butter and sugar together until pale and fluffy.

2. Gradually stir in the flour and ground rice. Mix well and press into a 18 cm (7') round sandwich tin.

3. Prick well all over, pinch up the edges with a finger and thumb. Mark into 8 triangles with a sharp knife and bake for about 40 minutes, until pale straw in colour.

4. Leave in the tin for 5 minutes, cut into 8 triangles, then dredge with caster sugar. Remove from the tin when cold.

RAMADAN

Officially, Islam recognizes only these two festivals, '**Eid-ul-Fitr**' and '**Eid ul-Adha**'. These are related to '**Ramadan**' (the month of fasting) and the '**Hajj**' (the pilgrimage to Mecca). Strictly speaking, these are not festivals, but are two of the five pillars of Islam, which are the basic duties all Muslims follow throughout their lives:

The five pillars are:

Shahada - the profession of faith. '**There is no God (Allah) but God, and Muhammad is the Prophet of God.**' All Muslims must publicly recite this at least once in their life as evidence of their faith.

Salat - prayers must be said five times a day every day, with congregational prayer on Friday.

Zakat - the giving of alms to the needy. This is another obligatory religious duty. Laws lay down the exact amount that each Muslim must give.

Saum - fasting during Ramadan. This means abstention from food, drink, smoking and sexual activity from dawn to dusk every day during the lunar month of Ramadan. It forms the background to the Eid festival.

Hajj - the pilgrimage to Mecca to pray for forgiveness on Mount Arafat and to visit the Ka'ba or Cube in the centre of the Grand Mosque. The origins of this great monument are unknown. Legend tells us that a great black stone which forms part of the eastern corner of the building was brought by Gabriel to Abraham, and that the stone now bears the imprint of Abraham's foot.

The stone was originally white but has turned black because of its contact with the impurity of the world. Every Muslim must try to make the pilgrimage at least once in their lifetime.

FASTING

Fasting is the duty of every Muslim over the age of twelve during Ramadan. They fast between sunrise and sunset each day. Food and drink may only be taken before dawn and after sunset. People who are old, sick, pregnant or nursing children do not have to fast. Extra time during this month is spent in the mosque at prayer and in reading the Qur'an, especially during the last ten days.

'Help me not to indulge myself, O God;
Rather make me ready to deny myself some pleasures;
And, as I do so,
May I think of my responsibilities towards others,
And feel myself nearer to you'

EID UL-FITR

The great family festival of Islam is Eid ul-Fitr, the festival of fast breaking, which marks the end of Ramadan, the month of fasting.

For three days there is plenty to eat with special foods and lots of parties. This is a time of joy because of the spiritual fulfilment of the fast. Everyone visits friends and relations, and cards and presents are exchanged. It is also a time for giving to the poor and every family sets aside a sum of money to give away.

The day always begins with prayer (salat). The men take a bath, put on their new clothes and go to the mosque for prayers.

The fast ends at sunset, and to open or break the fast, dates are eaten. There are two reasons for this. One is for religious reasons and the other for the nutrients they contain. This is followed by a milkshake with ice cubes and topped with ice-cream to give a very cooling effect. Eid cards, greetings and presents are exchanged.

EID UL-ADHA

This is the festival of sacrifice, and it is the second major festival in Islam. It is celebrated two months and nine days after '**Eid ul-Fitr**.' The festival takes place on the day following the pilgrim's visit to Mount Arafat, outside Mecca.

On the morning of '**Eid ul-Adha**', everyone has a bath or shower and puts on new clothes. Then they all go to the mosque or prayer hall for communal prayer. After the prayers there is a sacrifice of many sheep or goats, followed by a feast. The sacrifice is in memory of Abraham, who offered a sacrifice after building the Ka'ba in Mecca.

MAWLID AL NABI

This festival is the Muslim celebration of the birthday of the Holy Prophet Muhammad. He was born in Mecca, in about 570 AD.

THE LIFE OF MUHAMMAD

Muhammad's father Abdallah died before he was even born. His mother Amina died when he was only six years old. So he lived with his Grandfather. When his Grandfather died, he lived with his uncle Abu Talib.

When he was young, Muhammad was a shepherd but later on he worked with his uncle Abu Talib as a merchant.

He married a woman called Kaddija and they had four daughters and two sons. His love for his family set an example striven after by many Muslim men.

Muhammad became very troubled by the social and spiritual corruption of the society in which he lived. All around him he saw poverty and oppression, violence and cruelty.

He would go off into the desert around Mecca for long periods of time to meditate. It was during one of these pilgrimages at the age of forty, that he received his first revelation from God. He was overwhelmed by a vision of the Angel Gabriel (Jibril) who commanded him:

'Recite! In the name of the Lord who has created everything, and created man from a clot of blood.'

At first he thought he was possessed by demons, but soon Muhammad received many more revelations through Gabriel over a period of twenty-three years. Soon he began to recite them, as commanded, to a growing band of followers.

Muhammad couldn't write, and the revelations were not written down in their entirety until twenty years after his death. Before that they were preserved by **'reciters'** (qurra) who were skilled in memorising thousands of words and repeating them word for word. It is these revelations that now form the Qur'an, Islam's sacred book.

Muhammad established the first Muslim community in Madina and, after his death, his followers continued to spread the Prophet's message.

THINGS TO DO

EID CARDS

At Eid al-Fitr many Muslims send each other greeting cards. There is a picture on the front, and a special message inside. The message is often in Arabic which reads from right to left, so the card is folded on the right-hand side.

<u>YOU WILL NEED</u>

Card, bright crayons

<u>METHOD</u>

1. Fold the card in half, keeping the fold to the right-hand. Choose one of the designs as shown and colour in.

2. Write '**Sal Mubarak**' in the card which means Happy New Year, or '**Best Wishes for the Happy Eid**', or '**Wishing you the Blessing of Eid**.'

Eid Mubarak in Urdu is written like this:

عید مبارک

A MOSQUE

<u>YOU WILL NEED</u>

Silver and gold paper cut into squares, large sheet of paper, glue

<u>METHOD</u>

1. Draw the outline of a mosque and decorate the dome with the gold paper and the rest of the mosque with the silver paper.

2. Take five pieces of paper and write the five pillars of Islam and place them round the mosque.

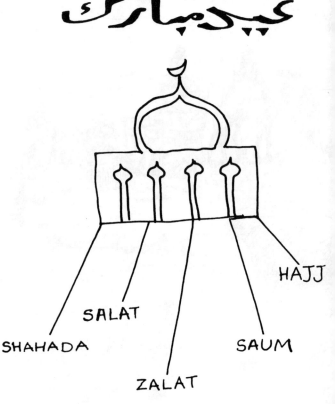

SHAHADA SALAT ZALAT SAUM HAJJ

NEW CLOTHES FOR EID

The holy Qur´an lays down the following rules about how to dress at all times:

Clothes must be loose.

They must be made of material that cannot be seen through.

Girls and women must cover their whole bodies except for the face and hands.

Boys and men must cover at least that part of the body between the navel and the knees.

YOU WILL NEED

Very large sheet of paper, material, glue, black or brown wool, pencil, small box, raisins, sultanas, nuts and dried apricot, crépe paper.

METHOD

1. Draw the outline of a Muslim boy and girl. For the hair, cut the wool into small strips and glue to the head. Draw a face.

2. Glue the material to the body to make the loose clothes.

3. Cover the box with crépe paper and glue as shown. Fill the box with the dried fruit and nuts.

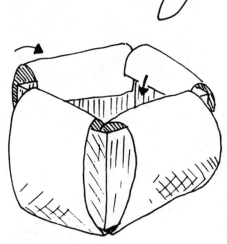

Suggested Songs: **Prayer to the Prophet Muhammad, Khushir Din (A Beautiful Day)**, from **Festivals (all the year)**, by Jean Gilbert, published by Oxford University Press. **Wahawi ya Wahawi (Ramadan is Come)**, from **A Musical Calendar of Festivals**, published by Ward Lock Educational.

COOKING

At the end of the fast of Ramadan, special dishes are prepared, and the table is spread with all sorts of delicacies. Spicy foods like meat or vegetable pastries (Samosas) are often eaten, and sweet foods like Sewiyaan. Sweet Samosas are also eaten which are filled with desiccated coconut and cream.

VEGETABLE SAMOSAS

YOU WILL NEED

Pastry

110 g (4 oz) plain white flour
25 g (1 oz) margarine
1 tablespoon cooking oil
1 teaspoon baking powder
3 tablespoons water
pinch of salt

Filling

25 g (1 oz) fresh or frozen peas
2 teaspoons garam masala
1 tablespoon cooking oil
1 teaspoon ground coriander
1 teaspoon ground cumin
3 tablespoons water

1/2 onion
1/2 carrot
1 large potato
salt and pepper

Oven temperature: 190 'C/375 'F/Gas 5

METHOD

1. Grease a baking tray. Sift the flour, salt and baking powder into the mixing bowl. Melt the margarine and add to the flour with the oil. Gradually add the water until a dough forms. Place the dough on a floured surface and knead.

2. Divide the mixture into 2 or 3 pieces. Roll each one out into a square and put to one side.

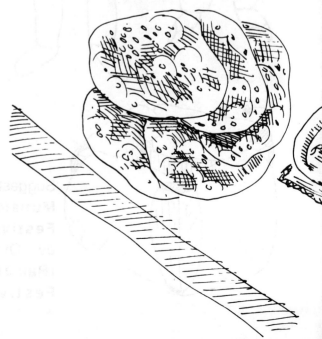

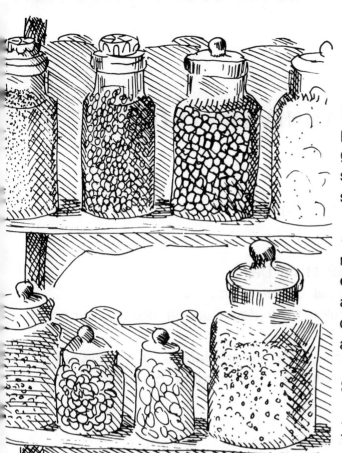

3. Peel and finely chop the onion, dice the potato and carrot, and fry in oil. Add the peas, garam masala, coriander, cumin, water and salt and pepper. Bring to the boil and leave to simmer until the vegetables are cooked.

4. Drain, then place a spoonful of the cooked mixture on each square of pastry. Brush the edges of each square with water and fold into a triangle. Brush each samosa with cooking oil and place on the baking tray and cook for about 20 minutes or until golden brown.

SEWIYAAN

YOU WILL NEED

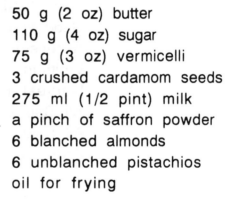

50 g (2 oz) butter
110 g (4 oz) sugar
75 g (3 oz) vermicelli
3 crushed cardamom seeds
275 ml (1/2 pint) milk
a pinch of saffron powder
6 blanched almonds
6 unblanched pistachios
oil for frying

METHOD

1. Heat the butter and crushed cardamom seeds in a saucepan until the butter has melted. Fry the vermicelli for 5 minutes. If pale vermicelli is used, the frying should turn them brown.

2. When the mixture has cooled, add the sugar and milk and bring to the boil. Lower the heat and put the lid on the pan, stirring occasionally to prevent sticking.

3. Uncover the pan and cook the mixture until dry. Add the saffron and stir well. Serve garnished with shredded almonds and pistachios.

DATES OF FESTIVALS AND ANNIVERSARIES

BUDDHIST Lunar

Every three or four years there is an additional eighth month which brings the calendar back in line with the solar year.

Late May - early June	Wesak, Full Moon Day
July 13th-15th	Bon, Festival of the Dead
Around July	Dhammacakka, the day Buddha first preached

CHRISTIAN   Part lunar, part solar. Christmas is a solar date - it is always December 25th. Easter is a lunar date and follows the Jewish lunar calendar.

January 6th	Epiphany, Twelfth Night
February - March	Ash Wednesday, the start of Lent
February - March	Shrove Tuesday and Pancake Day
March - April	Palm Sunday and Holy Week
March - April	Good Friday and Easter Sunday
April - May	Ascension Day
May - June	Whitsun
Around 15th October	Harvest Festival
November 1st	All Saints' Day
November 2nd	All Souls' Day
December 25th	Christmas Day

HINDU

The Hindu calendar is divided into twelve months according to the movements of the moon, and each month is divided into two halves. The first half begins on the day after the new moon and is called **'bright half'**. The second half begins on the day after the full moon and is called **'dark half.'**

April - May	Vaishakha, New Year
June - July	Ratha Jatra, Chariot Festival
July - August	Raksha Bandhan, Brother and Sisters
July-September	Janmashtami, Birth of Lord Krishna
Early September	Ganesh's Birthday,
Late October	Dashara, Autumn Festival
Late October-early November	Diwali, Festival of Light
November - December	Navanna, New Rice
Late Jan - early February	Saraswati Puja
February/March	Mahashivaratri, Festival of the God Siva
March 22nd	Holi, Festival of Colour
Late March	Ramanavmi, Birthday of Lord Rama

JEWISH Lunar

Every three years an extra month is added to bring the calendar back in time with the solar year. Because of the extra month, festivals vary in their dates on the Western calendar.

February 2nd	Tu B'Shvat, Tree Planting in Israel
Late February - early March	Purim, celebrates the deliverance of the Jews from a terrible plot
Late March to April	Pesach, Passover
Late May - early June	Shovuot, Pentecost
Mid-late September	Rosh Hashanah, New Year
Mid-late September	Yom Kippur, Day of Atonement
Mid December	Hanukkah, Festival of Light

MUSLIM Lunar

The Islamic calendar loses 10-11 days every year against the Western calendar, but no extra month is added so festivals move backwards every year.

April 15th 1991	Eid-ul-Fitr, a time for prayer
May - June	Lailat ul-Qadr
July	Al Hijra
July - August	Eid ul-Adha, celebrates the end of the pilgrimage to Mecca
October - November	Mawlid Al-Nabi, celebration of prophet Muhammad's birthday

SIKH Lunar

Each month starts with a new moon, and falls between their ordinary months.

January - February	Basant
February - March	Hola-Mohalla, Spring Festival
April 13th	Baisakhi, The Founding of the Khalsa
May - June	Martyrdom of Guru Arjan Dev
Mid November	Birthday of Guru Nanak
December - January	Birthday of Guru Gobind Singh

AMERICA

2nd Sunday in May	Mother's Day in U.S.A.
14th	Flag Day in America
July 4th	American Independence Day in U.S.A.
Last Thursday in November	Thanksgiving in America
December 26th - January 1st	Kwanzaa (African - American)

CHINA

January 21st - 20th February	Chinese New Year
February 4th - 6th March	Teng Chieh, the Festival of Lanterns
April 4 or 5	Ch'ing Ming, Festival of Pure Brightness
June 5th	Ch'u Yuen, Dragon Boat Festival
July - August	Festival of Maidens
September 1st-9th	Chinese Kite Festival
September	Moon Festival

JAPAN

January 1st-3rd	Oshogatsu, New Year
February 3rd	Setsuban, the start of spring
April 8th	Buddha's Birthday
May 3rd	Hina-Matsuri, Dolls Festival
May 5th	Kodomo-No-Ho, Children's Day
July 7th	Tanabata, Japanese Star Festival
Mid September	Tsukimi, Moon Viewing,
September	Respect for the Aged
November 15th	Shichigosan, Feast Day
November 23rd	Thanksgiving day